Samantha
Martin

BUSH
TUKKA
Guide

EXPLORE
AUSTRALIA

Contents

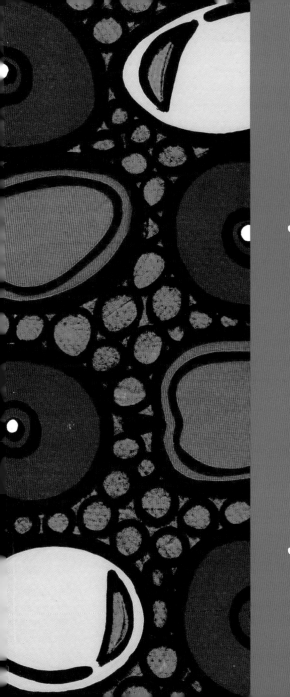

Introduction

About the author

Samantha Martin is a descendant of the Kija and Jaru from the east Kimberley region of Western Australia. She was born into a long line of traditional hunters and gatherers, and had the opportunity to learn from her family how to eat off the land and surrounding waters. Samantha understands the nutritional properties and diversity of Australian bush foods, and now wants to help others introduce native foods into their kitchens. She is also passionate about sharing her knowledge of basic survival skills, including how to hunt, prepare and cook bush foods. Known as the 'Bush Tukka Woman', her four-part documentary *My Bush Tukka Adventures with Samantha Martin*, has been screened on SBS/NITV (National Indigenous TV station) for the past six years.

Introduction

My name is Samantha Martin. My skin name is Nywarru. My Aboriginal name is Nyadbi, which means tall white gum tree, and I am a descendent the Kija and Jaru in the East Kimberley region of Western Australia. I am very proud to say that my greatest blessing is being born into the world as an Aboriginal woman.

Being Aboriginal plays an important part in my life story. My love of bush tukka became evident to me when I was nine years old. My mother Nancy Martin was the person who taught me the value of bush tukka and gave me the knowledge of the changing seasons, and of what to eat and what not to eat in the bush. I would watch in great awe how my mother would hunt, gather and prepare bush tukka; how she knew exactly what to eat and where to find it. My mother would show me the shape of the different leaves and the barks of different plum trees and berry trees and she would tell me to memorise that plant for next time. She explained to me that there are many poisonous plants and animals, and showed me how to identify some of them. She also told me to taste with the tip of my tongue, not to put the whole food in my mouth because the toxins can cause extreme upsets in the stomach and sometimes death. In general, however, bush tukka is one of the most undervalued foods due to the lack of education about its uses and nutritional values.

You just have to look at pictures of how lean and muscular our ancestors were back in the days of traditional bush living to see how well their diet provided them with energy and nutrients to live. But over a short period of time, bush tukka became a thing of the past; a process too hard to do – the preparation it takes to hunt, gather and prepare some bush tukka is almost exhausting to even think about. It's so much easier to 'hunt and gather' food in aisle 5 of a supermarket, where it is already skinned, cut, and packed all nice and neat.

I have seen our cultural values of hunting and living off the land diminish before my eyes. But I can understand why our society turned its back on bush tukka: how can traditional hunting compete with commercial convenience? I also, however, blame a lot of it on the lack of education and awareness about bush tukka.

In this book I wanted to introduce bush tukka to you, so that you can identify different bush tukka when you are out in the bush, and appreciate the way Aboriginal people lived off the land but also with great respect for the land. I also hope that you find some bush tukka that you will be inspired to try in your own cooking at home. I love cooking. And I love cooking with bush tukka. So I have also included some of my favourite recipes to get you started. I hope you enjoy them!

Samantha Martin, the 'Bush Tukka Woman'

Teachings from my ancestors

Shared knowledge

Australia is a unique and diverse country in every way – in history, culture, geography and climate. The knowledge about this great country that was shared with me by Aboriginal elders, is the richest knowledge I could ever wish for.

The Australian bush is home to a lot of edible and poisonous plants and wildlife. To identify edible plants in different areas around Australia is not that easy, but it is a good survival technique to have. To some people all trees and all shrubs look the same. Those who know what to look for however can identify what a plant is just by looking at the texture of its bark, the colour and shape of its leaves, and the flowers that grow on that plant.

It is also helpful to know about the diverse changes in the landscape, where these plants grow best and what climates they thrive on. Aboriginal people carefully observed the environments they lived in. Some flora and fauna can only be found in certain parts of Australia, for example: the boab tree (*Adansonia gregorii*) can only be found in the east Kimberley region of Western Australia due to the perfect dry temperature and rugged terrain of that area; the bunya trees (*Araucaria bidwillii*) only grow in the much colder climate of high hinterland tropical country in south-east and northern Queensland and northern New South Wales. Both the boab and bunya trees are hardy trees and need no maintenance once established. They will grow and reproduce in their perfect environments. As for the fauna of our country, the witchetty grubs can only be found in central Australia and the freshwater eel is only found in the waters along the east coast.

Indigenous background knowledge

Aboriginal people have survived and lived off this land for tens of thousands of years and have learned how to respect and acknowledge the land and the animals. Before the early settlers arrived in Australia, there were well over seven hundred different Aboriginal language groups sharing this country. Each clan had their own hunting

tools, hunting and gathering techniques, dreamtime stories, language, and spiritual rituals. Each clan respected each other's boundaries and would on many occasions seek right of passage to trade tools, traditional foods, and sometimes women; this was one way of ruling out inbreeding within clans.

The clan is an important unit in Aboriginal society. A clan is a group of about 40–50 people with common totems. It consists of groups of extended families. Generally, men born into the clan remain in the clan territory. This is called a patrilineal group, but everyone in the clan knew their own roles in keeping a peaceful and balanced family, from the men's responsibilities of hunting larger animals like kangaroo, emu, plain turkeys to the women and younger men's responsibilities of hunting the small animals such as goanna, small rock wallabies, fish to echidnas. The women had other responsibilities as well such as gathering bush berries, plums, bush medicines, looking after the children and the elders.

My ancestors knew how and where to hunt for food and never took anything more than they needed. What they killed they ate; they never let anything go to waste. They used the teeth, bones, hide, sinew, and feathers, for making tools, costumes, or weaponry. They also gave reverence to the life of the animals they killed, to take on the strength or the speed of that animal. But if the animal was someone's totem, that person was not allowed to eat it.

Spiritual totems

Most Aboriginal people will be given a totem. This means that they take on the spirituality of the animal, plant or other object believed to be ancestrally related to them. Totems can be represented through nature in the form of a large rock, tree, hill, river, or other landform. A lot of Aboriginal art is connected with the imagery of the artists' totems.

Water

Australia is one of the driest lands in the world, but the Aboriginal nomads knew exactly where to find water. They knew how to read the signs to follow a flock of birds flying by, which would lead them to waterholes. They knew the underground bores and springs which they could use as reliable sources of water; sometimes they would cover the holes up with a huge rock or sticks and leaves to keep the animals from drinking and contaminating the water.

Plants

The high diversity of Australia's flora includes large numbers of species which are ecologically significant such as acacia, eucalyptus, melaleuca, grevillea and allocasuarina. Acacias tend to dominate in drier inland parts of Australia, while eucalypts dominate in wetter parts.

Australian vegetation also plays an important part of the ecosystem and can be a great reference for Aboriginal people, indicating where they should look for bush tukka. In the northern part of Australia mangroves, savannah and tropical rainforests offers a supermarket of bush tukka. Aboriginal people in these areas, and other areas throughout Australia, relied heavily on the life cycle and the mating season of plants and animals which affected their survival in the Australian outback.

Animals

In Australia there are more than 378 species of mammals, 828 species of birds, 300 species of lizards, 140 species of snakes and two species of crocodiles. Of the mammals, almost half are marsupials. The rest are either placental mammals or monotremes, which are mammals that lay eggs instead of giving birth to live young like marsupials and placental mammals.

Among Australia's best known animals are the kangaroo, echidna and emu.

Our land, our country

For thousands of years Aboriginal people have learnt how to adapt and survive in the diverse and sometimes inhospitable environments found across the vast Australian landscape, learning the simplest but most important survival skills of how to find water and food in the driest and most desolate lands. They had to learn how best to hunt wild animals with the few tools they had or those they made from the natural resources that were accessible to them. They learnt that not everything was edible and that some fruits, berries and nuts were highly toxic, but also that with time and a long, drawn-out process some of those fruits, berries and nuts became edible and could be used as an important staple of their diet. Today, Aboriginal people are still taught from an early age these skills of how to read the landscape; we are shown how to look for signs which show us when, where and how to find water and bush tukka.

The pure connection that an Aboriginal person has to this land is profoundly unique. When Aboriginal people are taught about our 'country', what we are referring to is the land which our ancestors have inhabited for thousands of years; the same land we were born in, and the creeks, rivers and valleys in which we hunt and gather and celebrate important life events; where an unseen and unheard vibration runs deep through the land that connects us to a songline that we feel when we are born.

This feeling is a knowing and a bond we have to our mother's, father's, grandmother's and grandfather's land. It spreads throughout our veins like the very blood that runs through them. We dream about our land. We miss our land when we are away from it. And we feel we have a custodian responsibility to protect and cherish our land, its stories and its existence as it has passed from one generation to the next for over 50,000 years.

The early explorers found it almost impossible to survive in this land. Unsure of what foods could be eaten, they were reluctant to accept any foods generously shared by the local Aboriginal tribes, thinking it would bring ill health because it was foreign to them. Most of the first Europeans perished from starvation and hunger. But this land is abundant with fresh water and bush tukka, and with a little awareness and education it can be an enjoyable experience to look for, and find, bush tukka growing in its natural environments.

Our landscape

One of the most important survival skills to have is an understanding of the different environments in Australia. The landscape changes dramatically and plays an important part within the Indigenous culture. To recognise the changes in the landscape is to identify the distinct meaning and relevance of each landscape and what foods and resources are available.

The southern half of Australia has a different landscape to the northern tropics of Australian. Southern Australia features a more Mediterranean climate and arid coastline with cold wet winters and hot dry summers. Most of Australia's northern tropical regions contain areas of mangrove swamps, rainforest, woodland, grassland and desert.

Desert people

The desert people of Australia are among the greatest hunters and gatherers. Having the skills, knowledge and understanding of where to find food and water in the desert is absolutely extraordinary. To a western person nothing grows in the desert because it's hot and has no life; there appears to be no food in the desert. They see nothing but red, hot sand and small, spindly shrubs. To the desert people, finding bush tukka is as easy as shopping in a supermarket: they know how to identify where they can find an underground spring, and they know where to dig for wild yams, and how to find honey ants, witchetty grubs, echidnas and sand goannas. Growing up in the desert is harsh. Dealing with the heat is difficult and exhausting. The climate changes from extreme heat during the day to freezing temperatures at night. Desert people rely heavily on their ancient, traditional practices of living off the land but the modern world also makes it easier to get around the desert in four-wheel drives, allowing these desert people to travel across their country more quickly than in the past.

Desert people have great dreamtime stories of their country. They depict hunting and gathering stories through their traditional dance and extraordinary, vibrant artwork. This shows how important it is for them to teach younger generations about what they eat off their lands and how they survive.

Rainforest people

Rainforest people are custodians of the forests. They have lived amongst some of the oldest living trees on our planet. Learning to survive in damp, cool, wet terrains, they have adapted to their thick, lush green surroundings. With fresh waterways readily accessible, they learned different methods of how to trap fish, freshwater prawns, freshwater eels and freshwater turtles, which provided them with the rich proteins and minerals they needed to be strong and healthy. The men and women would both participate in catching freshwater prawns by throwing handful of leaves from small waterholes (where the prawns live) onto the banks and grabbing the prawns before they scurried back into the water. They also used a certain plant, known as foam bark tree or (*Jagera psuedorhus*), to stun fish. They crushed the leaves, put them in their dillybags and soaked the leaves in still waterholes. This takes the oxygen out of the water and the fish would float to the surface where the rainforest people would gather them (the poison did not harm humans).

The rainforest people also delighted in hunting scrub hens and collecting their eggs from their nesting mounds, they made nets to capture the scrub hens by using strong fibres obtained from the inner bark of particular fig trees.

They also gathered and ate wild berries, plums, roots, seeds, nuts and yams when they were in season and only took what they needed.

Rainforest people were very clever during the wet seasons. During this time they moved towards drier environments to escape the wet, damp and cold landscape which became difficult to hunt food in. They would return to the rainforest in the dry season when they needed to cool down from the scorching heat.

Freshwater people

Freshwater people live inland from the coast, surrounded by vast lands. They rely on freshwater wetlands, swamps, rivers, creeks, waterholes and billabongs to catch many species of fish, freshwater turtles, freshwater eels and freshwater prawns. The freshwater people have a deep spiritual and cultural connection to these waterholes.

Many tribes around Australia share in the common dreamtime stories of the rainbow serpent, the creator of the rivers and waterholes. The rainforest people believe that the waterholes hold a powerful spirit, which sleeps at the bottom of the waterholes and should be respected and not disturbed.

Living by waterholes like rivers, creeks and billabongs offers a protected and peaceful environment for the tribes. They can fish on a daily basis and gather under the cool, shaded paperbark and eucalyptus trees. The women and children also spend time swimming and collecting freshwater mussels from the banks and freshwater prawns from the rivers. But they also understood that setting up their camps by waterholes also brought the danger of crocodiles, so they always kept a watchful eye for these large animals.

Saltwater people

Aboriginal people who live on the coastal fringes of Australia are generally known as saltwater people and their hunting is ruled by the sea and the tides, but they also have an impressive knowledge of the ocean environment. Saltwater people have a deep spiritual and cultural connection to the sea and the ocean, and they believe that if they disrespect the ocean, it will not provide them with fish. Saltwater people hunt in mangroves swamps, estuaries, rivers, beaches and along reefs. Coastal saltwater people delight in collecting different varieties of shellfish including oysters off the rocks, mud mussels and mangrove snails from the mangroves and cockles from beneath the sand and rock pools. They thrive on the diverse and abundant source of marine life.

Coastal people have different hunting tools so that they can spear fish, stingrays, crabs and turtles. They only hunt for what they need, never more than they could eat. Most of the shellfish and fresh fish were caught and cooked before it was eaten, but there are a few animals that are eaten fresh like mangrove worms and oysters, and turtle eggs were drunk to quench their thirst while they were out hunting.

The tropical zones

To understand the diverse climate and weather patterns in Australia you firstly have to understand the breakdown of the three tropical climate zones in northern Australia. This will give you a better understanding of the two main seasons which the northern people know the wet and dry seasons.

The zones are broken up into three parts:

Equatorial zone one

This area ranges from the tip of Cape York Peninsula to Bathurst, Melville Island and the north of Darwin in the Northern Territory zone.

Tropical zone two

This zone spreads right across the northern regions of Australia including Cape York (again), the top end of the Northern Territory, areas south of the Gulf of Carpentaria and the Kimberley Region in Western Australia.

Subtropical zone three

This zone covers the coastal and inland fringe from Cairns, along the Queensland coast and hinterland, to the northern areas of New South Wales, and the coastal fringe north of Perth to Geraldton in Western Australia.

The wet and dry seasons

Around the world everyone is familiar with the four seasons (summer, autumn, winter and spring) that change every three months. In the tropical zones of northern Australia there are only two key seasons. These seasons last for approximately six months each. The wet season, otherwise known as the Monsoon, starts its build-up of rain clouds around August but will commence its downpour of rain in November through to March. It is actually hotter than the dry season, with temperatures soaring between 30–50 degrees Celsius. This is caused by the high humidity and build-up of moisture in the air from the high volumes of water on the ground which was caused by extreme flooding.

The dry season on the other hand is what it states. Everything is so dry. This period also lasts for six months, commencing around April and lasting through to October. With clear blue skies, the temperature will reach around 20 degrees Celsius. But the land gets punished from the dry heat and the burning sun rays which dry up the land, grass and waterholes.

The build-up to the wet season lasts 3–4 months between the wet and dry. This is the humid time of the year, the time when everyone becomes edgy as they swelter and in the humidity and wait for the first rains to fall. People in the Cape York region call it the Mango rain – the first rain that comes to give the mango trees a drink while they start to bear fruit. People in the Kimberley region call it the silly season as people tend to do silly things due to heat exhaustion dealing with the prolonged humidity, which lasts all day and all night with no break. But when the rains finally fall it brings a welcome relief to all the people as well as the lands and animals as it cools everything down.

During extreme flooding in the wet season it's difficult to get around as the ground becomes soaked and boggy. This generally means hunting season is over for a few months. During this time of the year, Aboriginal people prepare themselves and stock up on food and water. But back in the days of our traditional ancestors this time of the year meant they would head for the high lands, up to the hill tops where they could reside in a warm and dry cave for months on end, and from where they can have a full view of the vast lands below them. They would sometimes travel down the hill on foot when they needed to go off hunting for large animals to feed the tribe.

The tropical zone in the Northern Territory and Kimberley areas rely on a basic seasonal calendar. This helps them to prepare for extreme weather such as cyclones, flooding, severe storms and bushfires which affect the road access in and out of the remote communities and towns. These

extreme weathers also impact the livelihood of the community and map out the hunting and gathering seasons for what is in and out of season.

Month	European season	Indigenous season	Descriptions
January	Summer	Wet season	The wet season
February	Summer	Wet season	The wet season
March	Autumn	Wet season	The end of the rains
April	Autumn	Dry season	The end of the rains
May	Autumn	Dry season	The hot start of the dry
June	Winter	Dry season	The hot start of the dry
July	Winter	Dry season	The cooler dry
August	Winter	Build up season	The cooler dry
September	Spring	Build up season	The humid times begin
October	Spring	Build up season	The humid times begin
November	Spring	Wet season	The first rains begin
December	Summer	Wet season	The first rains begin

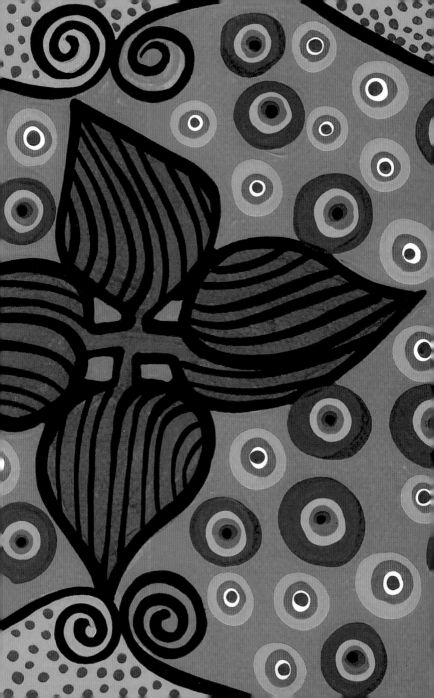

Plants

Billygoat plum 🍴 ➕

Aboriginal name/s gubinge or kabiny plums (Bardi tribe, west Kimberley, WA) **Botanical name** *Terminalia ferndinandiana*

Billygoat plum (also known as gubinge, kabiny, Kakadu plum or murunga) is a tree native to the tropical woodlands from north-western to eastern Arnhem Land, in the Northern Territory. It also grows in the east and west Kimberley regions, in Western Australia. A mature billygoat plum tree grows to 15m high, with creamy-grey bark and large, oval-shaped leaves. Up to 10–20 plums grow on one long stem. The plums are sometimes light yellow but mostly light green. They are an interesting shape, similar to an almond, about 2cm long and 1cm wide, with a very pointy end.

The billygoat plum tree flowers between September–December, with small, creamy-white flowers growing along the stems and producing a sweet aroma. The tree fruits from March–June.

Traditional use The Bardi people (from the Dampier Peninsula, near Broome in Western Australia) use every part of the gubinge tree, learning from their ancestors not to waste anything. From December–May, just after the wet season, the local Indigenous people are still harvesting the fruit to meet demands. They not only eat the fruit from the tree, but they also eat the tree's sap by cooking it in a bowl over hot coals until it hardens. The bark is also used as bush medicine by boiling it and applying the liquid to the skin to heal rashes, infected sores and sunburn. This liquid is also drunk as a tea to treat inflammation in the joints.

Other uses Billygoat plums have a sweet and sour flavour, very similar to dried apricots. They can be eaten raw or used raw in fruit salad.

Billygoat plums have become extremely popular within large health-food companies as a valued ingredient because they contain antibacterial, antiviral and antifungal properties, and much more. Billygoat plums reportedly have the highest concentrate of vitamin C than any fruit tested in the world. For example, an orange contains 53mg of vitamin C and a billygoat plum contains an average of 2907mg of vitamin C. Health-food companies are using billygoat plums or gubinge to develop an organic vitamin C powder, and are also looking to use it in the cosmetic industry for such things as soaps, shampoos, skin lotions and ointments.

Blue quandong 🍴

Aboriginal name/s guwandhaa (Wiradhuri tribe, central NSW), murrgan (Djabugay tribe, Kuranda, Far North Qld) **Botanical name** *Elaeocarpus angustifolius*

 Blue quandong trees are native to the rainforest areas of south-east Queensland and northern New South Wales. They grow well in the moist soil of subtropical rainforests, mostly around water systems such as rivers or creek lines, and are best known as the rainforest giants soaring as high as 40–50m into the sky. Aside from their height, they are easy to spot amongst the other rainforest trees because their long, glossy, dark-green leaves grow to an average length of 10–18cm. The leaves turn from green to a vibrant red colour just before they fall to the ground.

The flowers are clusters of bell-shaped, green–white petals, which start flowering in autumn–early summer and are a delicious treat for rainbow lorikeets.

The fruits are bright blue, growing up to 20mm in diameter with a thin layer of edible green flesh under the skin. Blue quandongs are not only popular bush foods amongst Indigenous people, but also among the native wildlife, especially flying foxes, woompoo pigeons and cassowaries. Legends have been told by rainforest people in Far North Queensland that the cassowary got its blue colouring from eating too many blue quandongs. Having a bitter, floury taste, the blue fruit are best eaten fresh; once they dry out they don't offer a pleasant flavour for your palate.

Traditional use The blue quandong stone is hard, brown in colour and has grooves all around it, like a walnut. It was used by local Aboriginal women to make necklaces, and over the past 10–15 years quandong necklaces have been coming back into fashion.

The fruit, although very dry in texture, keeps you hydrated for hours. Aboriginal women and children would scrape off the flesh by the river and make a paste out of it, which they ate when they needed to hydrate.

Other uses People have been known to pickle and jam blue quandongs, which offer a bitter, tangy flavour. It is great to use in stews with red meats because they sustain the bitter flavour better. But because it does not have a lot of flesh on it, it makes it very difficult to use in commercial cooking.

Boab nut 🍴➕

Aboriginal name/s jumuluny (Kija tribe, east Kimberly, WA)
Botanical name *Adansonia gregorii*

 Boab trees are a Kimberley icon, growing right across from the west coast of the Kimberley to the east, into the Northern Territory. Every boab tree is unique; they grow tall, skinny, fat and round. They range from 10–15m in height and 9–12m in width. The leaves are a bright lime–dark green and shaped like a star.

The boab tree drops its leaves in the dry season, and then commences a new growth around September–early October, ready to flower in November. The flowers are spectacular to look at; light cream in colour, they start as pods, then the petals peel back revealing long brushes of pollen stems which produce a magnificent perfume. The flowers open early in the evening and are pollinated that night, lasting only one or two days on the tree before falling to the ground.

The boab tree produces boab nuts, which are hard pods with a light brown fur that grows on the outside. This fur should be scraped off because it can cause itchiness if direct contact is made with skin. The hard pod is broken open to reveal the fruit, a white, powdery pith that contains at least 10–20 seeds (bigger nuts contain even more seeds). The powdery pith inside the nut, along with the seeds, is what can be eaten. It has a sherbet texture and a sour, tangy flavour.

Traditional use The boab tree is also known as the bottle tree among Indigenous people because of its unique, bottle-like shape. Indigenous people throughout the Kimberley used every part of the boab tree: they used the bark to make strong, thick twine; the trunk to produce water by banging it until it softened, then stripping off the stringy fibres and ringing them out to release the water; the fruit for food and medicinal purposes to treat gastro and intestinal blockages. The shells of the pods were used as cups to collect water, and as bowls and utensils.

To create a sweet treat, Aboriginal women and children would collect ripe nuts and break them open to expose the soft yellowish pith and seeds inside. The pith and seeds were then crushed and mixed with water and sugarbag droplets (see p. 19), and then eaten; it is very tasty. Young or unripe fruit were buried in warm ground to make them ripe and ready to eat (this was the more

Boab nut

traditional way of eating them). The seeds found inside the pith can also be dried and eaten like peanuts. The men preferred the boab nut young, while the inside is still soft and sticky. They would place the whole young nut on hot coals and let it roast through. It tasted very similar to roasted wild yams – sweet, warm and filling.

To this day Aboriginal people still carve on the boab nuts using a pocketknife or a sharp tool. These carved nuts are famous among tourists who like to take a little bit of Kimberley treasure home with them.

Other uses The fruit of the boab nut can taste sweet or sour, depending on how fresh it is; a fresh fruit has a sweet, tangy flavour. They have been used to make boab chocolates, muffins, bread and cakes. Dried boab flakes are sprinkled over salads to add a tangy flavour. You can make jams and chutneys using boab nuts.

People also sell boab roots commercially, promoting the benefits of its high fibre and high vitamin C content, as well as its richness in other minerals.

Bunya nut 🍴

Aboriginal name/s bunyi bunyi (Kabi Kabi tribe, Sunshine Coast, Qld)
Botanical name *Araucaria bidwillii*

Bunya pine trees grow in Far North Queensland, south-east Queensland and northern New South Wales; in subtropical rainforests and in the hinterland among moist soil, mostly on mountain-tops. Growing as tall as 30–45m, with rough-barked trunks, to protect them from the cold winds, and sharp-pointed, dark-green leaves about 2.5cm long. The bunya pines also produce large green cones about the same size as a football but weighing approximately 10kg.

The cones can be found during late January–early March. The female cone produces 50–100 bunya nuts, which grow inside beige kernels, held together around the stem of the cone by a waxy, white sap. To remove the kernels from the cone, simply pull them off from the base of the cone with your hands.

Bunya nut 🍴

The kernels are soft (but tough) fibrous packages which need to be peeled back to get to the actual bunya nuts. Each kernel contains one teardrop-shaped bunya nut, approximately 6cm long. The easiest way to get to the nut is to boil the kernels for up to 30 minutes, until the water turns slightly brown, or you can see each kernel develop a small split at the tip. You can then peel the kernels open with a knife.

Traditional use The Aboriginal word for bunya pine was *bon-yi*, which, over time, turned into *bun-ya*. Bunya nuts were a staple food of the Indigenous people living in south-east Queensland. They ate them raw or roasted them on hot coals. Every year in bunya season, bunya nuts were collected from all over the region to hold a bunya gathering and feasting. Many tribes would put aside their differences and gather in the mountains for their yearly bunya-nut feast.

Young Indigenous warriors would climb the rough-barked trees to get the young cones and then carry them all the way back down to the ground. The climb is extremely challenging because the tree trunk has hard, rough, very sharp bark that can slice your foot if you don't know the correct climbing techniques. The climb was done in ceremony and was taken extremely seriously; only the fittest of the warriors were chosen to climb the tree.

Other uses Bunya nuts are a great bush food and very versatile. When eaten raw they taste slightly sweet and are crunchy in texture; it is similar to eating a raw sweet potato. To cook the nuts, it's as simple as boiling or roasting them whole, or cooking them on the barbecue. Once they are cooked the bunya nut looks like a giant pine nut, but it is easier to open and tastes very similar to a chestnut, sweet with a floury waxy texture.

People have found many ways to introduce bunya nuts into their cooking. The nuts can be used in making soups, using the nuts to replace potatoes. The nuts can also be pickled or made into pesto, or used in beef casseroles, damper, scones, cakes and desserts such as biscuits.

Burdekin plum 🍴

Aboriginal name/s guybalam (Djabugay tribe, Kuranda, Far North Qld)
Botanical name *Pleiogynium timorense*

 Burdekin plum trees can grow as large as 20–30m in height and are predominantly found along coastal areas, creek lines and in rainforests areas in tropical Far North Queensland. They belong to the mango family.

Burdekin plum trees are distinctive looking, with a strong trunk (which is grey in patches) and dark, rough bark. They have long, rubbery-looking branches on which the plums grow in bunches of 2–10, sometimes more. The leaves range in colour from dark to light green, and grow to about 10cm in length and 4–6cm in width. Eight to 10 leaves grow on a single stalk, and the flowers are small, creamy-white constellations.

The plums are deep purple, almost black, and they grow to the size of a 50-cent piece, but can vary in size depending on the environment. The fruit grows in winter months. They have a thin layer of purple flesh which surrounds a large, hard, woody seed, and are quite tarty in flavour; the riper the fruit, the sweeter the flavour. But they do not ripen on the trees. Instead, they ripen from the ground-surface temperature when they fall.

Traditional use Burdekin plums were, and still are, very popular with local Indigenous people. They enjoy eating the tarty, tangy plums fresh or cooked. In the old days the women and children would crush the plums into a paste; because the fruit is made up of approximately 70 per cent water, it offered a great way to hydrate on long, hot days.

Other uses Burdekin plums are highly sought after by people in Far North Queensland who enjoy making jams, jellies, cakes and cookies from the fruit. They make great chutney, and savoury or sweet sauces which go well with pork, chicken, lamb and beef.

Burdekin plums contain vitamin C and are high in fibre and other natural minerals.

Bush onion 🍴

Aboriginal name/s yarrin yarri (Yawuru tribe, the Kimberley region, WA), merne yalke (Arrernte tribe, central Australia, NT), erreyakwerra (central Australia, NT), jurnda (Jaru tribe, western Kimberley desert, WA)
Botanical name *Cyperus bulbosus*

 Bush onion plants look like grass clusters, and grow in the Kimberley region of Western Australia and in central Australia. They are found in the coastal dunes and sand hills of the floodplains as well as on the fringes of saltmarsh flats.

Above the ground, the bush onion grows as a thin, spindly, vibrant green blade of grass that turns yellow when dry. It is best to gather the onions when the grass is yellow and dry. The small edible bulbs grow around the roots, so to find the bush onions you have to first identify the right grass blades, whether green or yellow in colour, then break the surface with a digging stick to loosen the sand. Once the sand is loose, gently spread the sand away with your fingers creating a raking effect. With the spreading of the sand, the small, brown bulbs will appear in clusters growing around the roots. Inside they are cream in colour and rubbery in texture and bland in flavour but filling; it doesn't take long before you gather enough to feed a family.

The onions can be eaten raw, or cooked in hot ashes. The tiny bulb also has a thin but tough brown husk around it that can be taken off easier after cooking in hot ashes. The bulbs become translucent after cooking them on the coals. They are very much like brown onions in shape and colour but taste totally different, more like pine nuts or chestnuts, and tasty after a while.

Traditional use Bush onions are an important bush food for Kimberley Aboriginal people, and the best time to look for yarrin yarri is after the wet season, around April–May.

When gathering bush onions Aboriginal people light a fire and then go off gathering so that the fire burns down to lovely hot ashes, ready for when they return with their buckets and buckets of onions.

There is a process for how to husk the onions to save time and energy, as it can be a tedious process if not done properly. Once the fire has died down the Kimberley Aboriginal people would remove the hot ash on top and place handfuls of onions in the remaining hot ash and

Bush onion

. . . .

cover it with the ash previously removed. They leave it for about 5 minutes and then with a stick they unearth the onions moving the ash to one side. They proceed to collect as many onions as their hands can hold, they then rub their hands together to create friction, rubbing the onions against one another until the husks start to peel away. Then they throw the onions in the air to let the husks blow away and catch the onions in their hands. They repeat this about 3–4 times, it's the only effective way to husk the pea-size onions.

Other uses Yarrin yarri was also crushed up and turned into a paste, flattened out to be made into a pita bread and then thrown back onto the coals to cook for about 10 minutes.

Bush passionfruit 🍴☠️

Aboriginal name/s yidiringgi (Jaru tribe, western desert, east
Kimberley, WA) **Botanical name** *Passiflora foetida*

Bush passionfruit is a weed-like vine that grows
all over other trees and shrubs. This climbing
vine is commonly found in the northern parts
of Australia, from the borders of Byron Bay
in New South Wales, across to Port Hedland in Western
Australia. The vine thrives on warm, humid–dry tropical
weather around rocky hills, swamps, creeks, riverbeds and
coastal areas – wherever there is a water system. The vine
and leaves are waxy in texture and will leave your fingers
with a strong, sweet scent if you touch them.

Each leaf has three points, similar to the common
passionfruit leaf. This distinctive vine can be recognised
by the delicate furry casing resembling a net, wherein the
passionfruit grows to the size of a grape. The casing starts
off lime green in colour and then changes to bright orange
or yellow. **Do not eat the fruit when they are green as
they are highly toxic at this stage.** Inside the bright orange

or yellow casing there is a soft, grey, juicy flesh with about 5–7 black seeds. Aboriginal people ate everything, the skin and seeds, but because the shell is very thin, the seeds can also be sucked out. The wild fruits are best during mid-summer, around December–February.

The flower on the bush passionfruit is one of the most stunning flowers you will ever see. It looks like a delicate orchid. Each flower is a wonderful mixture of white, light and dark purples, and light and dark greens.

Traditional use Wild passionfruit are a favourite treat amongst Aboriginal people. They were eaten freshly picked from the vines and were a refreshing treat on hot days.

Other uses Wild bush passionfruit are everywhere and are easily accessible to anyone who would like to introduce these sweet golden treats into their kitchen. They work well raw, on cheese platters or in fruit salads; just wash them and drop them in whole or squeeze the seeds over the fruit salad.

If you dry the flowers out, they make a great sleep-time tea.

Bush passionfruit is full of vitamin C and antioxidants, providing a natural source of vitamins and minerals to maintain a healthy immune system.

Bush sugarbag

Aboriginal name/s ngarlu (Jaru tribe, western desert, east Kimberley, WA), guku (Yolngu tribe, Arnhem Land, NT)
Botanical name *Trigona* and *Austroplebeia*

There are over 1500 species of native bees in Australia and only 10 of those species are non-stinging bees, also known as social native bees. These bees produce bush sugarbag. Social native bees are about half a centimetre long, and blue-black in colour, with hairy, extended back legs, which carry the nectar and pollen. They are known to be found in warmer, tropical areas such as the northern half of Western Australia, the Northern Territory, Queensland and the northern and coastal areas of New South Wales.

Social native bees are attracted to native plants, and can live in artificial nests but need to have good, warm insulation; hollow logs make the best nests. Different non-stinging bees make different types of entrances to their hives depending on their environment; some entrances are narrow, others are wide. When you spot a honey nest, tap

Bush sugarbag 🍴➕

on the trunk to find the hollow point before you chop the whole tree down, look for a small brown waxy 'nose' or mound – their entrance into the tree. When you have located the entrance take an axe and slice the branch to reveal the opening, you will see the yellow larvae and then the honey pods.

Bush sugarbag is dark brown in colour and can be found in tree hollows where social native bees have made their nests. These bees are not aggressive, but if you disturb their nests, they will swarm around you and stick to your skin or hair.

Social native bees produce and store small amounts of bush sugarbag with dark brown wax. The bush sugarbag is tangy in flavour but has a delicious bush-flower aroma. The honey pods are round and very different to the commercial bee pods; they look like a bunch of round, golden-brown grapes stacked neatly next to each other.

Traditional use Indigenous people are able to spot a beehive high up in a tree, it can be as simple as seeing a small, waxy hole at the end of a branch or spotting the small black bees, which look very similar to flies, flying in and out of the hole. I have known my aunties to follow a single bee to its hive, which is a difficult thing to do out in the middle of the bush, but they found the hive and were rewarded with the most delicious, sweet, silky-smooth honey.

Indigenous people used the honey as a little sweet treat, but they also used it to treat sore throats by eating it, and infected wounds or skin rashes by smearing it over the infected areas.

Sugarbag is highly prized, especially by the men. They would harvest the dark brown wax to use when making their tools and weapons such as axes, spears and woomeras. They would prepare the wax by chewing and squeezing it to remove the honey. Then they would use the wax to attach the axe heads to the handles by heating it and moulding it over the wooden handles. They would place the axe head on top and then, using natural twine, bind the wax and the axe head in place to make the axe.

The wax was, and still is, used for the mouthpieces on didgeridoos, or *yidakis* as the Yolngu people of north-east Arnhem Land call the didgeridoo.

Other uses Bush sugarbag can get very messy when being collected in the wild, but if you can strain the honey and collect enough of it, it is good to use in the same way as common honey: as a spread on bread, or to add to your cooking, salads, cereals or in teas. Bush sugarbag can also be used in a medicinal way as it contains antibacterial properties. A teaspoon of sugarbag honey can treat sore throats, chest infections, colds or flus.

Bush tomato 🍴➕☠️

Aboriginal name/s kampurarpa (Pitjantjatjara tribe, central Australia, NT)
Botanical name *Solanum centrale*

The bush tomato is a small desert plant, approximately 30cm in height, with grey-to-bronze leaves and attractive mauve–blue flowers. It grows well in the hot, dry climates throughout the central deserts: from Tennant Creek in the Northern Territory, to Marla in South Australia and the east Kimberley in Western Australia.

In the red sandy desert, these plants grow quickly after summer rains, mainly from dormant rootstock which can last for many years between favourable seasons. The plants also respond and grow rapidly after soil disturbance (along roadsides) or after bushfires. In the wild they fruit for only two months, and the dried fruits are collected in late autumn and early winter.

There are 100 species of wild tomatoes in Australia, however only six are known to be edible. **The other Solanum are highly toxic. They contain high levels of solanine which is known to be poisonous.** If you are not familiar with this plant, do not experiment with it as the poison can cause severe stomach aches, vomiting, diarrhoea, and it can be fatal.

Also called kutjera, these desert raisins, are known for their sweet and slightly tangy flavour. They are the most well known and certainly the most consumed species of bush tomatoes. Kutjera grow between 1–3cm in diameter, and are yellow when ripened.

These days, bush tomatoes are grown commercially by Aboriginal communities in the deserts of central Australia. Using irrigation, they have extended the fruiting season to eight months, offering a longer supply of bush tomatoes to the commercial culinary industry.

Traditional use Kutjera are an important bush food. This arid-lands fruit has been a staple food of the Indigenous desert-dwellers of central Australia for many thousands of years. The traditional harvesting method is to collect the sun-dried fruits off the small bush in the autumn and winter months. In its dried form, bush tomato can be stored for several years.

Bush tomato 🍴➕☠️

Traditionally kutjera offered a treat for the women and children, who ate the fruit fresh. The fruits were believed to build immunity, while also nourishing and hydrating the body from the heat. But if too many are eaten, it can act as a laxative.

Aboriginal people also used the roots of this plant to treat toothache. The roots were baked in ash and then peeled, crushed and placed on the aching tooth.

Other uses Bush tomato has a strong sun-dried tomato flavour and aroma when dried. It is just delicious in recipes with white or game meats such as fish, chicken or pork. It also offers a lovely Indigenous twist to homemade dukkah or pasta sauce, and adds a great smoky flavour to marinades for pork, beef ribs, steaks or roasts.

The dried fruit is normally ground and used as a seasoning, rather than used whole. It is particularly suitable for use in casseroles and soups, giving a rich, robust flavour. This bush food has a variety of uses but should be used fairly sparingly. Its strong flavour can quickly overpower more delicate food, especially if used in quiches, or with eggs or cheeses. The bush tomato compliments the traditional ingredients used in Mediterranean-style cooking such as eggplant, olives or capsicum. Ground bush tomato is best kept cool and dry, and has a considerable shelf life.

Cluster fig 🍽️ ➕

Aboriginal name/s ngalga-yarrubadjal (Djabugay tribe, Kuranda, Far North Qld) **Botanical name** *Ficus racemosa*

Cluster fig trees are magnificent, reaching up to 30–35m high, with large, green leaves. They are known as majestic giants, and grow along riverbanks, riverine forest and in much drier environments that have underground water systems. They grow mostly in Western Australia, Northern Territory, north-east Queensland and south-east Queensland. Playing an important part in the ecosystem, cluster fig trees provide food for humans and animals, natural medicines and shade along the waterways.

Cluster fig trees are easy to recognise because the figs grow on the branches and trunks in clusters. The clusters change colour at different times, from light green to yellow, orange and then to red when the fruits have ripened. The figs are produced around

Cluster fig 🍴➕

September–December. The figs that grow on the external root system of the tree are much sweeter in flavour and, like common figs, have hundreds of little seeds inside. But the cluster figs are often infested with insects and larvae, so best check before taking a bite.

Traditional use This remarkable species of tree offered several different methods for survival to the Aboriginal people who relied on cluster figs not only as a main food source, but also used other parts of the tree for medicinal purposes and to make tools and canoes. They would scrape off the inner bark and boil it in water to produce a liquid that was good for treating diarrhoea. They would also hollow out the soft, inner part of the trunk to make canoes and coolamons because the wood is light, strong and waterproof.

Other uses The cluster fig tree will provide great shade in your garden and will attract an array of wildlife from birds to insects, but ensure you do not plant a cluster fig tree near buildings, paving, sewer lines or houses, as their aggressive root system does grow extremely fast and will damage whatever is in its way.

Cluster figs work well in jams and chutneys. You can also bake them, then drizzle them with a syrupy sauce and add ice-cream on the side for a delicious dessert.

Conkerberry

Aboriginal name/s piriyalji (Kija tribe, east Kimberley region, WA)
Botanical name *Carissa lanceolata*

 Conkerberries, also known as bush currants, are native mainly to the Top End and central Australia, but are also found in the Kimberley in Western Australia, and around Cape York in Far North Queensland. In a hot, dry climate it grows on a wide range of terrains and soil types. However, in wetter parts it tries to keep confined to relatively wetter areas only.

The plant is a multi-stemmed shrub, 1–3m high and 1.5–4m wide. Its leaves are glossy green, narrow and 1–5cm long. It has hard thorns, also 1–5cm long. The white, star-shaped flowers, about 1cm wide, have a sweet scent and grow in December–January. The small berries, 1–2cm long, appear in February–March. They turn dark purple, or even black, when ripe and have a sweet taste.

Conkerberry 🍴 ➕

This plant also becomes a weed in Australian grazing lands. It can multiply fast by natural layering. In such cases, it becomes a menace and is difficult to control, even with herbicides.

Traditional use Aboriginal people frequently eat conkerberries, as their sweet taste is refreshing.

The conkerberry tree was also used in other ways by Aboriginal people. They burnt the wood of the tree and used the smoke created to treat colds and coughs by inhaling. The leaves were boiled and the liquid swallowed, also to treat colds. The orange roots were cut, chipped and burnt, and the smoke was used to keep bad spirits away from children up to their early teenage years. This smoke also chases away mosquitoes, and was placed on a fire when mosquitoes were in the area. The branches of the conkerberry tree were often used as a bush broom to sweep up around camp. And the V-shaped part of the branches was used to form the hook part of a woomera.

Other uses Conkerberries are still a native secret. They can be used to make desserts such as conkerberry cheesecakes and conkerberry scones, and can also be added to fruit salads.

Desert lime 🍴

Aboriginal name/s (not recorded) **Botanical name** *Citrus glauca*

Australian desert limes are from a tree species belonging to the citrus family. These trees grow inland, in dry areas like western Queensland, particularly around the Roma district in the south-west. They also grow in New South Wales and South Australia. They are the quickest citrus tree species in the world to set fruit after flowering. They have also evolved to protect themselves against grazing animals by growing sharp thorns. However, the trees cease to have any thorns on growth above the browsing height of large kangaroos!

Desert lime trees are slow-growing, like most of the Australian-native citrus species. The small, multi-stemmed, dense trees grow up to 12m high, and have slender, upward-facing leaves, 5–8mm wide. The limes grow to the size of grapes. Small, white flowers are produced around

Desert lime 🍴

August and the fruit ripens by November–December. The fruits look like tiny lemons with a porous rind and juicy, but sour, centre.

Traditional use Desert limes were eaten raw by Aboriginal people and stockmen to quench their thirst; stockmen would eat the fruit straight from the trees while mustering.

Other uses This interesting bush tukka is very easy to use. It has an intense, acidic flavour; it is said that it is difficult to simultaneously eat desert limes and smile!

Desert limes are considered a very healthy food with three times the amount of vitamin C found in oranges. They require no peeling, de-seeding or other preparation, and can be used in any product or process where 'normal' limes or lemons are used; the main differences being their small size, lack of peel and more intense flavour. They also have the valuable attribute of freezing without losing flavour or presentation characteristics when thawed for later use.

One of the best ways to use desert limes is when cooking fish in foil or paperbark; slice the desert limes in half and drizzle the juice over the fish. Desert limes can also be used in sauces, marmalades, pickles and chutneys. One of my favourite uses for desert limes is in desert lime sorbet. You can also try them in your favourite cocktail drink or punch, for a great look and wonderful lime twist.

The versatility of this fruit, its tarty, tangy flavours and its outback origins allow it to be admired by food enthusiasts.

Green plum 🍴➕

Aboriginal name/s taaluny (Kija tribe, east Kimberley, WA)
Botanical name *Buchanania obovata (Anacardiaceae)*

The green plums, otherwise known as taaluny trees, commonly grow in the eastern part of the Kimberley in Western Australia, and in the Top End of the Northern Territory. Growing as tall as 5–10m, with round-edged, light-green leaves that are about 12cm long, these trees are found in rugged terrains close to creeks and rivers. The Kimberley region has two seasons, a dry season and a wet season. The dry season lasts from May–October, and the wet season lasts from November–April. Taaluny trees start to flower in September (the middle of the wet season) with delicate, creamy-white flowers, and they start to fruit from October–April (from the end of the wet season until the end of the dry season).

The taaluny is a round, light-green plum, the size of a five-cent piece. The fruit has a hard, black seed inside and juicy, green flesh on the outside.

Traditional use Indigenous people in the Kimberley consider the taaluny a treasure. The women, men and children would spend hours collecting the fruit, filling buckets and buckets. They would crush the flesh of the plums and create a paste to eat without the hard, black seeds getting in the way.

Other uses Taaluny was, and still is, used as a laxative to treat constipation. Rich in vitamin C and fibre, this little fruit offers a natural, healthy way to boost your immune system. The seeds can also be crushed up to get the nut inside which tastes very similar to a macadamia nut.

This little fruit also offers a delicious sweet and tangy treat on a hot day.

Lemon aspen 🍴➕

Aboriginal name/s (not recorded) **Botanical name** *Acronychia oblongifolia*

Lemon aspen seems well-adapted to surviving, growing and having a generally healthy, green appearance in a wide range of environments. It grows best in tropical–subtropical rainforest, particularly in highland areas and will tolerate both full-sun and semi-shade, although it prefers well-drained and fertile clay loam soils, with a sunny aspect and extra moisture when young. Lemon aspen can be found in north-eastern Queensland, occurring naturally from Cooktown to Mackay, but it can be grown much further south.

This tree grows up to 2m high and has dark-green, elliptical leaves. Flowering in summer–late autumn, the delicate, white flowers have been observed to last only a few weeks, but they give off a stunningly sweet scent.

The small, cherry-sized fruit is about 1.5–2.5cm in diameter. It is a pale-lemon colour, and has a tough, star-shaped core – textured much like an apple core, and similarly like an apple, with very small black seeds. The thin layer of flesh is slightly spongy. The fruit exudes an incredible tropical-citrus aroma (much more so when fresh) and has a sharp citrus flavour with lemon characteristics. Lemon aspen needs to be picked slightly under-ripe.

Traditional use Aboriginal people ate lemon aspen straight off the tree, enjoying its citrus flavours. They also squashed handfuls of the fruit into a container to extract the juice, which they drank to boost the immune system and to clear sore throats. The juice was also used as an antiseptic by rubbing it on sores or boils.

Other uses The flavour of lemon aspen is extremely strong – 100g of lemon aspen equals something close to the juice, zest and pulp of about six large lemons. It works best in dressings, marinades and dishes where a little can be added at the last minute for a burst of freshness. This versatile fruit can be used in 100 different ways such as making jams, jellies and juice. Whole lemon aspen fruits or just the juice can be used in pastries, desserts and sauces. The pulp from juicing can also flavour shortbread, lemon aspen mayonnaise or lemon aspen vinegar. It is suggested that the leaves can also be used for flavouring. They are excellent in curds and salad dressings. This fruit has high levels of anti-oxidants and B vitamins.

Lemon myrtle 🍴➕

Aboriginal name/s djulungunu (Djabugay tribe, Kuranda, Far North Qld)
Botanical name *Backhousia citriodora*

A healthy lemon myrtle shrub grows to about 1–5m in height and 1.5m in width. It grows naturally in the cool, wet climate around northern and southern Queensland, and northern New South Wales, where it has been cultivated for commercial and private use. Sadly, the plant does not grow wildly anymore.

The shrub has an attractive, healthy look with full, lush branches that hang gracefully, holding long thin leaves which grow heavily on each branch creating that full, bursting appeal. In autumn the shrub will grow stunning clusters of creamy-white flowers, which give off an intensely sweet, lemon fragrance. The shrub itself does not bear fruit. The leaves are the hero of this plant and are becoming a feature of Australian cuisine.

Traditional use Aboriginal people used this plant to keep hydrated by sucking on the leaves. This provided them with nutrients, vitamins and minerals, which fought off diseases and gave energy to the body. They also made use of the high antibacterial properties in the leaves by chewing them or crushing them into a paste to rub on sores or boils. The leaves were also used as an insect repellent by burning them to create a thick smoke which kept the mosquitoes away.

Other uses Considered as the 'queen' of the lemon herbs, lemon myrtle is now one of the most popular and versatile native bush plants. Its benefits range from flavouring savoury and sweet dishes to healing uses.

In cooking, lemon myrtle leaves can be used in a similar way to bay leaves in marinades, soups, stews, casseroles and roasts. The flavour can be intense and overpowering, but used properly it will complement chicken, beef, lamb and kangaroo dishes. For desserts, try using the dry, crushed leaves in cheesecake fillings or bases, apple crumble bases, biscuits or cakes. Once you do introduce lemon myrtle into your kitchen, you will quickly become hooked as it brings a unique flavour to dishes.

The plant also contains anti-inflammatory properties which can be used to treat swollen fingers, toes and joints by sucking on the leaves to release their natural oils, or by making a tea from them. To drink lemon myrtle as a tea,

Lemon myrtle 🍴 ➕

pluck a handful of leaves and add to a pot of boiling water; wait until the water and the leaves turn slightly brown. The tea can be drunk warm or cold, and you may like to add a teaspoon of honey for extra flavour or sweetness.

Lilly pilly 🍴

Aboriginal name/s daguba (Cadigal tribe, formerly of the area currently around Sydney, NSW) **Botanical name** *Acmena Smithii*

The common pink lilly pilly is known as Australia's leading bush tukka. Unpruned and depending on its environment, lilly pilly trees can grow up to 15–20m high, but most people use it for hedging; with its shiny, green, pointed leaves, 3–6cm long, the plant makes a great shield for privacy. Lilly pillies grow well in rainforests in north and south-east Queensland, and throughout New South Wales and Victoria.

Lilly pillies flower from October–March. The flowers appear as white, fluffy, thumbnail-sized clusters and give off a sweet scent. They are extremely attractive to bees.

Lilly pilly 🍴

Lilly pilly fruits develop from October–May. They grow into pear-shaped berries which are red, purple or white, and grow to 13mm in length. Each berry contains a single seed, 4mm in diameter.

There are many, many species and cultivars on the market.

Traditional use Aboriginal people on the east coast and in the hinterland and rainforest areas relied on lilly pillies as a staple of their diet. They commonly referred to the berries as 'medicine berries' because they provided vital minerals and vitamins to fight against colds and flu, keeping their immune system healthy and strong.

Lilly pillies were mainly picked and gathered by women and children, providing the children with a sweet treat throughout the day.

Other uses Lilly pilly berries can be eaten fresh off the tree or gathered and then frozen to use at a later date. They contain high levels of vitamin C and are long lasting; they keep for up to 1–2 weeks after being picked, and even keep their colour. This is one reason that they have become popular in commercial kitchens.

These pink, tart berries are great in fruit salads, adding that little extra tangy crunch. They are also fantastic in smoothies, jams, chutneys, ice-creams, savoury and sweet sauces, and even candy.

Mountain bush pepper

Aboriginal name/s (not recorded) **Botanical name** *Tasmannia lanceolata*

Mountain bush pepper is a versatile little bush treasure. This small tree grows 2–5m high and 1–2m wide, with attractive, bright-red stems and glossy, dark-green leaves. It grows naturally in rainforest areas, in the cool, wet climate around southern New South Wales, and throughout Victoria and Tasmania.

It produces cream-coloured flowers from October–January, depending on its location. The berry-like fruits are 5–10mm in diameter, beginning dark red and turning shiny black when ripe in summer or autumn. The berries generally appear only on female trees, though plants of both sexes contain flowers. Plant growth is moderate-to-fast under the favourable conditions of a cool, wet climate.

Mountain bush pepper

Traditional use Traditionally mountain bush pepper was used to treat infections by eating it. Sore gums and tooth aches were treated by crushing the pepper berries into a paste with a bit of water and applying the paste to the affected areas. The paste has a bite or sting to it but it does kill the bacteria in the infection.

Other uses Mountain bush pepper has a strong earthy flavour with a hint of heat. You can add ground mountain bush pepper leaf to olive oil for dressings and tapas platters. It adds a unique flavour to dukkah, and also any roasted meats or vegetables. A small bowl of ground mountain bush pepper placed in the centre of the table can be 'pinched' over soups and sauces, much like black pepper.

Native basil

Aboriginal name/s (not recorded) **Botanical name** *Ocimum tenuiflorum*

Native basil is an aromatic plant, which grows wild on rocky ledges and rugged surfaces in the dry and hot climate of Queensland and the Northern Territory.

Native basil is an ankle-high, woody herb with small, pale-green, pointed leaves that are 3–5cm long. The plant has soft, delicate, fragrant, lush foliage that is extremely hardy, so it grows well through summer and throughout the year in warmer areas of Australia. The plant can be mistaken for a weed, but if you crush the leaves in your hand you will be able to distinguish whether it is native basil by its woody–sweet basil scent.

Native basil 🍴➕

Traditional use Indigenous Australians used this plant for medicinal and ceremonial purposes. For medicinal purposes, the leaves were crushed into a paste and applied to infected wounds, boils and on skin infections until they would dry up. It also worked as a painkiller and was used to fight off infections as it contains traces of antibacterial properties. In ceremony, the dried leaves and branches where used in a smoking ceremony by adding them to hot coals to create a smoke used to cleanse bodies or places of bad energies.

The women would also use native basil as a form of perfume. They would lightly crush the leaves to release the sweet aromas and then rub the paste on their bodies and through their hair to smell sweet.

Other uses Native basil can be used in the same way as Asian or sweet basil. It is a great base for many dishes including pesto sauce, which is a combination of garlic, olive oil, pine nuts, basil and shavings of parmesan cheese. You can also add native basil to your pasta dishes, and your Asian dishes such as stir-fries or curries.

Native finger lime

Aboriginal name/s not known **Botanical name** *Citrus australasica*

Native finger limes are another little treat which the Australian bush produces. A mature tree can grow about 6–10m high. The small tree is now native only to rainforest areas of south-east Queensland and northern New South Wales, as their habitat has been destroyed by farming and commercial land developments.

Finger limes are a treasure to local Indigenous people and other Australians who know about them, but in the past decade the demand for finger limes has grown steadily because they have been discovered on a more grand scale.

Native finger lime 🍴➕

They are now being heavily promoted in commercial kitchens around Australia and the world as citrus caviar, citrus gems and citrus pearl drops.

The finger lime tree is spindly and quite spikey. The leaves are small, dark green, shiny and delicate, and can grow from 1–2cm long and half a centimetre thick. The tree is deeply layered with thorns, which grow to about 3cm long, longer than the leaves.

Native finger limes grow in the shape of fingers, hence its name. On average a healthy finger lime can grow as long as 6–12cm and as thick as 2cm. The lime's pulp comes in an assortment of colours from lime to dark green, bright to light pink, blood orange to light orange, to pearly yellows. You can generally tell the juice colour from the colour of the skin.

The delicate flowers are small and white, and have a sweet scent. The tree starts flowering from June–early October, but in warmer climates the tree may flower sporadically throughout spring and summer. Fruit development can last as long as five months from flowering to harvesting, with the fruit maturing between December–May.

Traditional use Finger limes have been a food source for Indigenous Australians for thousands of years. They were also used to fight off any viral or bacterial diseases. Finger limes were used as an antiseptic for infected sores or boils by crushing the pulp and applying the juice to the wounds.

Other uses Finger limes are highly sought after by chefs in commercial kitchens and restaurants all over the world. These citrus gems are not only used in sweet and savoury Australian dishes, but infusing finger limes into Asian cooking has become a huge trend over the last few years.

Finger limes have become increasingly popular in chutneys, jams, marmalades, marinades, and savoury and citrus sauces. They are also used as a garnish, especially for beverages such as champagne and cocktails.

Finger limes are ideal with fish (raw or cooked), oysters, chicken, pork and salads. They are best eaten fresh but can be frozen to use later.

Native gooseberry 🍴

Aboriginal name/s kirliny (Kija tribe, east Kimberley, WA)
Botanical name *Physalis minima*

Gooseberry shrubs are often found in dry soil in areas near water systems such as riverbanks, on the edges of swampy areas and, most often, around cattle yards. They grow in the Kimberley region in Western Australia, Arnhem Land in the Northern Territory, and in the Cape York region in Far North Queensland.

The shrubs look very spindly, with bright, dark-green leaves and small, delicate, white flowers. They can grow as high as 1–2m. Each shrub has hundreds of small, paper-thin pods which change from green to a golden-yellow colour when they ripen. As the fruit ripens inside the paper-thin pod, the pod will change from soft and moist to brown and dry, with a crepe-paper-like texture. When it ripens and turns yellow, the pod, with the fruit inside, will fall to the ground. Inside the paper-thin pod is a small tomato-like fruit. Growing 1–2cm in length, the fruit, like the pod, changes from green to a bright-yellow colour as it ripens. The fruit matures between December–February.

Traditional use Indigenous people still collect gooseberries in the wild today. They are a popular delicacy for Aboriginal people, especially women and children who will spend hours sitting in one spot collecting buckets and buckets of fresh gooseberries from shrubs and from the ground.

Other uses Gooseberries are delicious eaten raw. They are sweet and taste very similar to a cherry tomato, with a slightly tangier aftertaste. These little berries are known to contain high levels of vitamin C.

Gooseberries all around the world have been a popular fruit in home kitchens. They are great in pies, salads, tarts, and gooseberry jams are a personal favourite. They can also be dried out and then crushed into a powder which is lovely to add to marinades and savoury, meaty dishes like stews and barbecue meats, or you can use it with seafood.

Native Australian gooseberries are also making their way into commercial kitchens in Australia. They're used mainly in desserts and work particularly well with other berries (including strawberries), apples and melted dipping chocolate.

Native guava 🍴 ➕

Aboriginal name/s bolwarra (Dharawal tribe, formerly of coastal area now known as the Sydney basin, NSW) **Botanical name** *Eupomatia laurina*

Native guava is a large spreading shrub growing 3–5m high. It has multiple trunks and glossy, dark-green leaves which grow between 6–12cm long, on 1cm thick vine-like branches. In the cooler winter and spring weather the foliage takes on a red–bronze colour. It grows well in the coastal rainforests of Far North Queensland and as far south as Victoria.

Flowering begins in spring and summer with lily-like flowers, 2.5cm in diameter, producing a sweet scent. However, each flower only lasts one day. The bud of the flower has a pointy cap, exactly like a eucalyptus bud. The flowers are pollinated by small brown weevils, which are attracted to the sweet scent.

The fruit is green in colour and grows in an urn shape, 2–3cm in size. The fruit ripens in winter and is ready when it is soft to squeeze. The creamy pulp is edible and very sweet; it has lots of seeds just like a guava.

Traditional use Indigenous rainforest people used the native guava leaves to treat diarrhoea, sore throats, vomiting, stomach issues and menstrual pains by simply boiling the leaves and drinking the liquid. The leaves were also used as an antiseptic on inflamed wounds or sores.

Other uses Native guavas are used in savoury and sweet dishes in commercial kitchens. They are also a favourite in the common household and are used in jams, chutneys and even for juicing.

You can buy guava leaf extracts and essential oils to alleviate inflammation and candida, and to assist in fighting germs and infections.

Rainforest tamarind 🍴

Aboriginal name/s biliybiliy (Djabugay tribe, Kuranda, Far North Qld)
Botanical name *Diploglotis smithii*

Rainforest tamarind is a thin tree growing to a height of 15–20m. It is native to south-eastern Queensland and northern New South Wales, and occurs naturally in wet, tropical rainforests. These trees can still be found growing in the wild, along coastal lowland around the north coast of New South Wales and on the Sunshine Coast and the Gold Coast hinterland in Queensland.

Native tamarinds are related to the Asian lychee family but certainly don't taste like lychees. Despite its name, the native tamarind is also not at all related to the common tamarind. It is a tall tree with large, rounded, green leaves, which are almost leathery or waxy-looking. The rainforest tamarind flowers in summer, producing small, delicate, creamy flowers.

The fruit grows in clusters and is ready to harvest in autumn. It hangs gracefully in a light-brown casing, holding three vibrant-red seeds. Its flesh is sour and tangy, very similar in flavour to green mango.

Traditional use Indigenous people gathered the native tamarinds every year. They offered a delicious treat for the men, women and children as they ate them raw. The women and children would sit by a river or creek and crush the fruit off the seeds. Then they would add water to the crushed fruit, creating a refreshing, tasty beverage.

Other uses Just like common tamarind, native tamarind can be made into jams, chutneys, and sauces for savoury, sour and sweet dishes. Native tamarind works well with chicken, pork, lamb and beef, especially in Indian and Asian dishes like curries, stews and stir-fries. The tangy, sour flavour can also work extremely well in baked dishes such as cheesecakes, biscuits and slices. It also makes refreshing cordial.

Native tamarind is full of vitamin C and natural minerals, offering a great way to boost your immune system.

Sandpaper fig 🍴 ➕

Aboriginal name/s djaribat (Worimi tribe, the Great Lakes coastal region, NSW), Yanggi (Djabugay tribe, Kuranda, Far North Qld), yimarlji (Kija tribe, east Kimberley, WA) **Botanical name** *Ficus fraseri*

The hardy sandpaper fig trees are looked upon as a weed, but to the ecosystem in which it lives these trees serve as an important food source for birds, caterpillars, butterflies, fruit bats, flying foxes and many other animals. These trees grow well in a warm, dry climate around water systems, riverbanks, rainforests and creeks. They are found in the northern parts of Australia and along the east coast from Mackay in Queensland, through New South Wales and just into Victoria near Mallacoota. A mature tree can reach about 8m high, but along coastal edges the trees grow quite small, about 2–4m, due to the high winds off the coast. The sandpaper fig flowers and fruits from spring to early summer and the fruit matures from December–February.

The name, sandpaper fig, comes from the texture of the leaves which are rough and harsh – exactly like sandpaper. The fruit are small, round and fig-like. They go from green to a deep-maroon colour when ripe, growing to about 1–2cm, with light hair particles on the outer layer.

The fruit is sweet and moist with hundreds of little, brown seeds. Like a fig, the outer layer is soft and sweet, and the tiny hair particles on the outer layer are fine to eat. The leaves are dark green and grow to about 5–15cm long.

Traditional use The local Indigenous people commonly consumed sandpaper figs as they were a sweet, nutritional treat. But the tree was more than a food source. The men used the leaves to sand back their tools and weapons, such as boomerangs, spears, coolamons and axe handles, to a smooth surface.

The thick, white tree sap was, and still is, used to treat the itchy symptoms and skin infections of ring worms by applying a thin layer over the ringworm scars.

Other uses Sandpaper figs are sometimes found on menus in commercial restaurants, served up as delicious desserts, cooked in the way that common figs are: roasted, baked or pan-fried in butter and syrup.

Sugarleaf 🍴

Aboriginal name/s pinkany (Kija tribe, east Kimberley, WA)
Botanical name *Glycaspis (Glycaspis) brimblecombei*

Sugarleaf are lerps, which are tiny, white, transparent shells or sometimes little fluff balls about 2–4mm long. These sweet white lerps are produced predominantly on eucalypt leaves by tiny, yellow, sap-sucking psyllid beetles, which use the lerps or droplets for protection. The sugarleaf are essentially made of sugars and starches extracted from the sap and expelled by the bugs. If you look closely at the white shells you will notice a similarity to fairy floss, and you will see the minuscule insects that are responsible for producing these little sweet sugar droplets. Sugarleaf can be found on gum trees and grey ironbark leaves, usually close to riverbanks. They are produced at the end of the dry season, just before the wet season.

These lerps are also referred to as 'sugar bread' and are eaten by simply running the leaf between your teeth; don't worry about eating the insects, you don't really taste them.

Traditional use Indigenous people really enjoyed eating sugarleaf, and they continue to enjoy them today. Children would collect and indulge in these sweet treats in between playing in their local waterholes.

Other uses The old people in the east Kimberley used sugarleaf to sweeten their tea. They would gather a whole branch and shake it onto a sheet to gather the sugarleaf.

Wattleseed 🍴 ☠

Aboriginal name/s merne ntange arlepe (Arrernte tribe, central Australia, NT) **Botanical name** *Acacia victorea*

Acacias, with their enormous diversity of species and forms, cover the length and breadth of the Australian continent. Indeed the wattle flower is the well-known emblem of Australia, and is represented in the green and gold worn by Australian athletes. Although not all acacias are suitable for human consumption (some contain high levels of toxins), they have been a mainstay in the diet of Indigenous Australians for thousands of years because Indigenous people knew the importance of preparing the seeds of certain species to eliminate the toxins by roasting them in hot coals.

Wattle trees are shrubby-looking trees, growing as tall as 5–6m. The branches are spindly and covered with spikey thorns up to 1cm long, and long, slender, light-green leaves growing 4–8cm long. They prefer hot and dry temperatures. Because of this, they are mainly harvested in the wild. The seeds of the acacias have very hard husks, and when they fall to the ground, they will last for up to 20 years in their natural environment, usually only germinating after bushfires.

Flowering begins in August and continues into December, depending on the region in which they grow. Each flower stem holds clusters of flowers with up to 12 flowers in each cluster. The flowers first appear a pale yellow then change to a vibrant yellow.

Seeds are best collected when they are dry and turn dark brown, generally in January, February and March. The seeds were crushed into flour between flat grinding stones, and cooked into cakes or damper. Even the green seeds of some species were eaten after baking in the hot coals.

Traditional use Harvested by the Aboriginal people 6000 years ago, seeds from the wattle plant were sought out as a versatile and nutritious addition to their diet. Because their hard outer casing protects the seed during long periods of dormancy on the ground, wattleseed has provided Indigenous Australians with a rich source of protein and carbohydrate in times of drought.

Though the plant is a member of the traditionally poisonous *Acacia* species, Aboriginal people discovered

Wattleseed 🍴☠

over 40 different edible varieties. The green pods were eaten raw, or dried and milled into flour for baking. Aboriginal people would collect the seeds and winnow them from their pods in coolamons or wooden bowls. The seeds would then be ground into a paste on a mobile grindstone (like a mortar and pestle) and mixed with water to form small, flat cakes. These cakes were baked in the coals of a fire and then eaten or stored for later use. Anyone who has spent time in Australia's deserts will have seen the old grindstones out in the sandhills where Aboriginal women used to sit and prepare their meals. The Aboriginal people also often cooked their food in ovens made by digging a hole in the ground and putting hot coals and hot rocks into it.

Other uses Wattleseed has to be considered the unsung hero of Australian native foods. It is very nutritious, containing potassium, calcium, iron and zinc, all in fairly high concentrations. With a low glycemic index, they are good for diabetics, providing a steady stream of sugars that do not produce sudden rises in blood-glucose levels. Wattleseed also has more protein than rice, pork or chicken. Research has been done to investigate the possibilities of Australian wattleseed being used as a famine-relief crop in African countries because it grows in deserts which typically have very poor soil, little or no water, and yet it produces an abundance of high-quality food each year.

Today, wattleseed is dried and roasted in a similar way to coffee but with a particular temperature profile. It is then specially ground to produce a highly versatile and nutritious flavour and later crushed to create extracts and a powder used in cooking and for making espresso-type coffee. The flavour of wattleseed is described as being reminiscent of hazelnuts and chocolate with hints of coffee. This makes wattleseed an ideal seasoning for ice-creams, nutty-flavoured butters, sauces and coffee beverages. Roasted ground wattleseed has a diverse number of uses in the kitchen, from baking to a thickening agent for sauces and casseroles. By roasting wattleseed, the most delightful aroma of nutty fresh roasted coffee is released and can be used as a beverage on its own or as an addition to chocolate or desserts. The flowers (without stalks) can also be used, typically in pancakes, scones and scrambled eggs or omelettes, in the same manner as elderberries.

Wattleseed is available online as an extract and a ground spice.

Animals

Black bream 🍴

Aboriginal name/s wulam (Djabugay tribe, Kuranda, Far North Qld),
jampinparuny (Kija tribe, east Kimberley, WA)
Scientific name *Acanthopagrus butcheri*

Black bream are a very common fish, mostly
found in fresh water. Do not mistake it
for saltwater sea bream, although they are
related. Black bream are golden brown when
in the water but their scales turn black once out of the
water, which is why they are called black bream. They grow
to 60cm long and weigh 4kg on average. They are caught
mainly in freshwater estuaries, rivers, creeks and billabongs,
but they prefer to swim under overhanging branches
among the branches of fallen trees, and in the bottom of
deep water holes.

In summer and early autumn the sperm and eggs are released into the water and the juvenile and adult bream find refuge in the upper level of the estuaries, but they often get washed downstream when the first rains fall in late autumn.

Traditional use Black bream is a treat among Indigenous people. Small and easy to catch, black bream is often caught and cooked straight out of the water (with scales and guts, so nothing gets wasted) on the coals for 5–10 minutes. Once it's cooked, they just peel the skin off to reveal the white, steaming-hot flesh. It tastes slightly sweet.

Other uses Bream is becoming as popular as barramundi, but it does not grow as large as barramundi. Black bream fillets are soft and white, and best cooked on hot coals, pan-fried, steamed or poached. Cooking bream whole is the best way to maintain its sweet flavour. It is especially delicious when cooked with Asian flavours.

Bustard bird 🍴

Aboriginal name/s wawun (Djabugay tribe, Kuranda, Far North Qld), kere artewe (Arrernte tribe, central Australia, NT), kipara (Luritja tribe, western desert, west and south of Alice Springs, NT), danimila (Larrikia tribe, land in and around Darwin, NT) **Scientific name** *Ardeotis australis*

Bustard birds, also known as bush turkeys (to Aboriginal people) or plains turkeys, are large ground birds that roam the grasslands, woodlands and open plains, mainly across the northern and central parts of Australia, where the climate is warm and dry.

The bustard bird can grow as tall as 1.5m, and has a wingspan of 2.5m. An average male can weigh 6.5kg. Female birds are smaller and more slender than the males. In appearance, the bustard bird has a mostly dull-brown body and speckles of black and white markings on its wings. Its head is crowned with black feathers and its neck and the bottom half its body is grey, which helps it blend in with its surroundings.

Traditional use Bush turkey has played an important role in the diet of Indigenous people throughout the Kimberley, the central desert, and Far North Queensland. It is still eaten today.

Bush turkeys also play an important part in the dreamtime stories. Many Indigenous people have totemic spiritual connections with the animal, and are allowed to paint the animals in their art.

As hunters of larger animals, Aboriginal men hunted the bush turkey using weapons like the spear and woomera. The woomera allowed the spear to be thrown faster, harder, more accurately and over longer distances.

When the men brought the bush turkey back to camp, the women and children were responsible for preparing it for cooking. It was then cooked on the hot coals, allowing the protein, omega fats and oils to remain in the flesh. It can become quite dry or tough in texture if overcooked. The flesh of the turkey is deep red, not white like common turkeys, and the flavour is very gamey.

Other uses Bush turkey has not yet hit the commercial food industry. In fact, these birds are now protected in some parts of eastern and western Queensland, although Indigenous people are still allowed to hunt them.

Bustard bird 🍴

There are various ways to cook bush turkey. It can be boiled with vegetables and made into a stew. It is especially wonderful when roasted with vegetables for 30–40 minutes (depending on its size). Bush turkey breasts can also be used in curries or stir-fries, served on a bed of hot rice and vegetables.

Common long-necked turtle

Aboriginal name/s nyangura (Ramingining tribe, Arnhem Land, NT), badjigal (Djabugay tribe, Kuranda, Far North Qld), tarntal (Kija tribe, east Kimberley, WA) **Scientific name** *Chelodina longicollis*

The common long-necked turtle gets its name from its neck, which is sometimes longer than its own body! It can grow up to 25–30cm in length. Its feet are webbed and very strong. It often uses its feet to tear apart its food. This turtle also has a sharp beak and strong jaw, so make sure you keep your fingers away from its beak.

Having dark-brown colouring allows this turtle to hide itself around rocks and mud to escape predators. It also buries itself in mudflats or dried-up riverbeds for protection during the dry season.

Like other reptiles, common long-necked turtles are most active during the dry season, travelling very long distances in search of new waterholes. During winter they lay dormant under logs and rocks, waiting for the water temperature to change before they go in search for food.

In the Kimberley region, they have Kimberley snake-necked turtles, a type of common long-necked turtle with the distinguishing feature of having very long chin barbells: thin, thread-like fibres that hang from the bottom of their chins. This is where their tastebuds are located; it helps them search for food in murky waters. Other fish that have the same feature are catfish, carp and some species of shark.

The snake-necked turtles are in abundance and are mainly found in dams, rivers, creeks and billabongs, as far west as the Fitzroy River system, as far north as Kalumbarru, Mitchell Falls, and the King Edward and Drysdale River systems, and in the eastern Kimberley region around Lake Argyle and the Ord River system.

Traditional use Aboriginal people enjoy catching and eating turtle. Aboriginal people in the Kimberley and north-east Arnhem Land prefer to eat turtle than fish, and delight in hunting and feasting on snake-necked turtles, as they are easy to catch in waterholes. When the people in Arnhem Land hunt snake-necked turtles they go to the cracked mud flats and walk along until they see a minuscule bubble amongst the hard, brown, cracked mud. Then they dig until they reach the turtle lying in the damp mud underneath, keeping moist and cool, away from the sun.

Not everyone can eat long-necked turtles. Some people have long-necked turtles as their totemic spiritual symbol. This means that before they were born, their life was of that animal, and they came to be born because their mother ate that animal and embodied its spirit. So to honour the turtle's spirit they must not eat it and if they catch it, they can either pass it onto their grandmothers to eat or let it go.

To cook and prepare a turtle Aboriginal people would prepare a fire and let the wood burn down to coals. When the coals are nice and hot, they place the turtle, shell-down, to cook the shell through. They do not gut the turtle before cooking it because this ruins the cooking preparation and also lets the juices out. Depending on the heat of the coals and the size of the turtle, it is cooked for 30–40 minutes. They keep a close eye on it to ensure that it does not become overcooked. When holes appear around the legs and the shell, the flesh inside is cooked. There are two ways to crack open the shell, one is to crack it with a hard object and then approach the meat from the top to the bottom. Alternatively the breast plate is cut away from the shell on the bottom, exposing the legs and guts of the turtle and keeping the juices in the shell.

Common long-necked turtle

The flesh of the turtle is pure white and has a similar texture to chicken breast and, in some parts, chicken thighs. But the turtle is much juicer and sweeter in flavour than chicken.

In the past turtle fats were rubbed on sick or weak babies' chests to give them strength. The oils offered healing minerals. Turtle offered a lot of protein and also gave strength to the men and the old people. Today it is still practiced that whenever you catch a turtle, you must give it to the old people first as a sign of respect.

Other uses Turtles don't really get used or cooked in a commercial manner; they are looked upon as more of a bush food that is best cooked in the bush. People in western cultures tend not to eat them because they think that they cannot eat something so cute or, much like whole fish (which many people prefer not to cook because they would rather someone else gut, scale and fillet the fish for them), many people find turtles too difficult to cook.

Crocodile 🍴

Aboriginal name/s baru (Galpu clan, Arnhem Land, NT) **Scientific name**
Crocodylus porosus (saltwater), *Crocodylus johnsoni* (freshwater)

There are 14 different species of crocodiles that have been identified in the world, but in Australia we have only two: freshwater and saltwater crocodiles.

Freshwater crocodiles are smaller, with a narrow snout; they are light brown with dark markings on the body and tail. They generally live in freshwater habitats, in the warmer waters of the northern parts of Australia, and feed mainly on fish and smaller vertebrates.

The more aggressive saltwater crocodiles are the largest living reptile, with a wider head and a broad snout. The saltwater crocodile is pale yellow and light brown when young, becoming dark green as an adult. Don't be fooled

Crocodile 🍴

by its name 'saltwater' crocodile, these giant water reptiles can survive in both fresh and salt water. The male can grow up to 7m long, and can weigh up to 2000kg; the female is generally smaller, reaching 3m in length. They live in mangrove swamps, lagoons, estuaries and low stretches of rivers throughout the northern parts of Western Australia, the Northern Territory and Queensland. So when you're taking a swim or strolling along the far northern beaches or rivers in Australia, be aware and cautious of crocodile-infested waters. Saltwater crocodiles will eat almost anything, from fish, turtles, wild pigs and wallabies, to kangaroos, buffalos, dingoes, live cattle, dogs and humans.

Traditional use Aboriginal people have been eating crocodile meat for thousands of years, and studies have suggested that eating the fatty, protein-rich meat may have helped early humans evolve bigger brains.

In Arnhem Land they call crocodile 'baru' and there is a strong totemic spiritual connection to the people and the land, which offers a mutual respect. There are many dreamtime stories from many different language groups around Australia about the crocodile; some tribes in Arnhem Land believe their ancestors crossed swollen rivers on the backs of these man-eaters.

Other uses Crocodiles are being farmed and are sold in leading butchers, commercial meat markets and online, with a wide variety of cuts available. Low in fat and high in protein, the crocodile's white meat is an increasingly popular bush food. It is featured on a lot of restaurant menus around the world. Sourced for its surprisingly tasty, tender flesh, crocodile meat has been used in curries, stir-fries, stews, sausages, pies and casseroles. Crocodile is best cooked rare to medium–rare to guarantee it retains its moisture, otherwise the meat can be tough and chewy. When cooking crocodile it is best to cook it in the same manner as pork or chicken as they have a similar texture.

Crocodile skin also is highly sought after to use in making handbags, belts, boots and shoes.

Desert sand frog 🍴

Aboriginal name/s wubun (Djabugay tribe, Kuranda, Far North Qld), nangalanangalal (Kija tribe, east Kimberley, WA)
Scientific name *Limnodastes ornatus*

Desert sand frogs can be found in the southern and western parts of Australia. Its natural habitats are freshwater lakes and sandy terrains; they like to burrow backwards into the cool moist layer of the sand, emerging at night to hunt for small insects. Small in size, reaching up to 5–8cm, they are blotchy in colour, from dark to light brown, cream to white. Their heads are small and triangular, and their bodies are usually flat but it puffs up when threatened.

Traditional use The Balgo people of Western Australia have a strong connection to their land. Although to the naked eye their land looks barren and dry, these desert people can go out during the day and come back with sand goannas, witchetty grubs and sand frogs. It does take hard work and travelling over lots of country to find them but they delight in gathering and eating desert sand frogs. When looking for the sand frogs, the women listen for the male sand frogs' calling from under the ground. This tells them where to dig.

To gather sand frogs, the women dig a hole as deep as their whole body to find one or two frogs. The sheer dedication of the women is remarkable. Once the frogs are caught and collected, they are thrown on the fire. They are cooked slowly on both sides for 5 minutes before being eaten.

They also make great fishing bait.

Other uses Like most bush tukka insects, desert sand frogs will not be found on the menu of restaurants. Sand frogs are only enjoyed by the traditional desert people whose ancestors have been eating them for thousands of years. These delightful little frogs are a delicacy to the Aboriginal people and taste very similar to quails.

Echidna 🍴

Aboriginal name/s ganyi (Wiradjuri tribe, central NSW), tjilkamata (Arrernte tribe, central Australia, NT), kernanjil (Kija tribe, east Kimberley, WA) **Scientific name** *Tachyglossidae*

About the shape of a football, echidnas are 30–45cm long and can weigh 2–7kg. These unusual-looking, egg-laying mammals are covered with coarse, long, black hair and sharp, yellow, black-tipped needles, which make them very difficult to handle. They have a stubby, hairless tail and long, sharp-clawed feet with which they can burrow through any ground surface, fossicking for food and water. They also find food with their long, sensitive nose. Once they have found food, they use their long, slim, sticky tongue to catch the ants or insects.

Echidnas are solitary animals. They are always found roaming on their own, but they can be found throughout Australia, especially around rocks, hollow logs, termite mounds and holes around tree roots.

Traditional use The Arrernte people of central Australia call the echidna *tjilkamata* and still go hunting for echidna today. Echidnas are very quick on their feet and are fast diggers, so if you find one you have to quickly roll it onto its back so it can't run away.

Before Aboriginal people cooked echidna they would carefully gut it, and then, with a skewer, close up the hole. To remove the needles they would boil the echidna in extremely hot water, then take a strong wire and create a loop around the feet to hold them while they scraped off the needles with a small axe or sharp knife. Once the needles were removed, the echidna was placed on the fire to burn off the remaining coarse hair, before placing it into a camp oven for 2–3 hours, until the meat is cooked right through and is bubbling with juices.

Other uses Echidnas have not hit the commercial markets, because it is seen to be cruel to eat the cute little echidnas, but this cute little animal has been a staple of Aboriginal people's diet for thousands of years and are not hunted in mass numbers.

Emu 🍴 ➕

Aboriginal name/s karnanganyjal (Jaru tribe, western desert, east Kimberley, WA) **Scientific name** *Dromaius novaehollandiae*

A large flightless bird, standing 2m tall, Emus have long, thin necks and soft, brown and grey, waterproof feathers. They have light blue skin around their neck, and piecing red eyes. This spectacular bird is related to the ostrich and is recorded as the second largest living bird in the world.

Emus can be found over most of mainland Australia. They prefer to roam around in dry savannah, bushy or scrubby woodlands and very dry areas.

Emus breed in May and June, and a female can mate with several males and lay several batches of eggs in one season. The eggs hatch after approximately eight weeks, and the young chicks are looked after by their fathers. They will reach their full size after six months. An emu can live for up to 10–20 years in the wild, if it survives its predators such as dingoes, hawks, eagles and humans.

Emus have strong, leathery feet with three toes and long, strong, black nails. Its nails are one of its only ways to defend itself. Emus have very long legs, allowing them to take a stride of up to 275cm, which makes them extremely fast runners, being able to sprint at 50km per hour.

Traditional use Emus are well-respected birds among Aboriginal people as they represent totems and skin names, and they hold an important place in Australian Aboriginal mythology. The Yuwaalaraay and other clans around New South Wales say that the spirits created the sun by throwing an emu egg into the sky. The Western Australian Indigenous people believe that the emu was created when a man was annoying a small bird; the bird threw a boomerang, severing the man's arms and turning him into a flightless emu. The emu was also believed to lie in the Milky Way, high in the sky looking over many Aboriginal language groups.

But in most tribes emu is extremely prized for its meat and feathers, which were traded with other groups. The men hunted larger animals; they had the endurance to walk long distances and the strength to use the weapons like the spear and woomera. The men figured out the emu's mating

Emu

calls and covered themselves in emu feathers to create a coat and used their arms as the neck, to lure the male emus closer before striking them with a spear or axe.

The women worked out that emu fat was good for the skin as a moisturiser, giving it a nice shine, but they also found that it helped to relieve aching bones and joints.

Other uses Emu meat is high in protein and low in fat. It needs to be prepared under strict control to ensure the meat holds it maximum quality. Emu meat is dark red and is best cooked fried or on a hot plate, like a barbecue, to retain it's juices and flavour. Emu meat is also best cooked medium–rare, similar to beef, lamb and kangaroo.

Emu oils are also used as a traditional Aboriginal medicine to treat weight loss, stretch marks, dry skin, rashes, eczema, wrinkles and ageing spots and much more. You can purchase the oils in markets or online. Gently rub it on the affected areas.

File snake 🍴

Aboriginal name/s witij (Gulpu tribe, north-east Arnhem Land, NT)
Scientific name *Acrochordus arafurae*

The file snake is a non-venomous water snake which is predominantly found in freshwater swamps, creeks and billabongs in Arnhem Land in the Northern Territory. You can identify a file snake quite easily as they are light–dark brown with a very thick body and a small, bulldog shaped head. The females are larger than the males; they can grow as long as 2.5m and weigh about 1.5kg.

File snakes are called file snakes because of their rough, spikey, scaly, file-texture skin. They mostly breed in the dry season and the females only breed once every few years

· ·

giving birth to approximately 20–30 babies, if the eggs survive attacks from crocodiles and birds.

They are also known as elephant trunk snake, Arafura file snake or wrinkle file snake.

Traditional use In the far north Arnhem Land region the Aboriginal women and children often hunt for file snakes, as they are a common bush tukka and are easy to find because these docile water snakes rest in the mud, in slow water or even on the banks of rivers. The women and children walk through crocodile-infested waters using their feet to feel around in the mud, when they feel something scaly, they reach down and grab the file snake and reach for its head to kill it instantly. They cook it whole on hot coals for 15–20 minutes. The flesh is white. It has a sweet flavour and a stringy texture; it's very similar to chicken but file snake has fattier flesh.

Yolngu people in north-east Arnhem Land have a spiritual connection to the file snake, not only as a food source, but also as an ancient totemic symbol. It features heavily in their artwork and stories as the rainbow serpent and lightning spirit: creator of the water holes, rivers, hills, valleys and mountains as it moved across the land.

Other uses File snakes aren't used in a commercial sense, as it's more of a traditional food. People still find it hard to gather the courage to eat snake as it's far from being fish or chicken. But file snake has high levels of protein and omega oils and is a clean, fresh meat to eat.

Freshwater catfish 🍴

Aboriginal name/s tanlinyi (Kija tribe, east Kimberley, WA)
Scientific name *Neoarius leptaspis* (boofhead catfish)

 Catfish is one of those fish that is not taken seriously. They are bottom feeders and dwell in still water, generally out of the current of the main channels. Its colour varies between grey or golden brown, depending on size and water environment. They grow to about 40–90cm in length. Catfish don't have scales, instead they have tough, leathery, sandpaper-like skin, which can make them difficult to handle. There is an important thing to know about catfish: they have sharp-edged spines in the dorsal and pectoral fins, which can penetrate the skin and inflict severe pain.

Traditional use Indigenous people cooked catfish raised slightly above the hot coals; not having scales to protect its flesh, it was best to cook it above the heat to retain the natural oils and keep the flesh moist. Most people turn their noses up at catfish, but Indigenous people really enjoy eating it, as it is fleshy and quite tasty.

Other uses Freshwater catfish flesh works well battered or grilled or in curries, stir-fries, fish stews and chowder.

Freshwater eel 🍴➕

Aboriginal name/s nyinggarra (Djabugay tribe, Kuranda, Far North Qld), lanyiny (Kija tribe, east Kimberley, WA) **Scientific name** *Anguilla reinhardtii* (Australian long-finned eel)

Freshwater eels are long and muscular, with brown–yellow skin when young, which eventually becomes mottled (for long-finned eels) or a dark-olive colour (for short-finned eels) as they mature. They are diadromous, which means that they migrate between the sea and freshwater, mainly for breeding purposes. Their natural habitats are rivers, lakes, estuaries and creek systems. They make the big journey into the ocean to spawn.

Long-finned eels are a more tropical species, while short-finned eels like to live in more mild waters, although both can be found up and down the east coast of Australia including South Australia, Tasmania, and as far as the Bass Strait Islands, Lord Howe Island, New Zealand and New Caledonia. They are well-travelled fish.

Freshwater eels are generally long and slimy, with snake-shaped bodies and small head. They usually have small pectoral fins to help them navigate along the river floor. They also have tiny, sandpapery teeth, so be careful when handling them.

Traditional use At Lake Condah in western Victoria, the Gunditmara and the Djab Warrung tribes say that their ancestors were not nomads, they believed that they lived in a village that farmed eels in swampland that had been excavated to create artificial channels and ponds, which were formed through lava flow. Evidence shows that in the 1800s Europeans moved in and drained the swampland but could not dismantle the natural channels created millions of years ago.

The Gunditjmara and the Djab Warrung people traded smoked eels with distant communities for other resources such as tools, weaponry and other foods. They used sophisticated methods of trapping eels by building grass-long eel traps with holes at both ends to allow the eels to swim into the nets and then exit the end one by one, where they were collected and killed and put in eel-proof baskets. The eels were slow cooked above hot coals, or smoked in a blackwood tree and the blackwood oil was taken and rubbed over aching bones or limbs, or drunk for medicinal purposes.

Freshwater eel 🍴 ➕

Other uses Eel is a delicacy all around the world and is farmed and cooked on a large-scale commercially. The skin is quite oily and fatty but the flesh is slightly pink, turning white when cooked. It has a very firm texture and a distinctive rich, fleshy flavour. Eels are high in omega oils and protein, offering vitamins such as A, B1, B2 and E.

Because it has a high oil content, it's best to cook eel in ways to eliminate some of the oil, like poaching, steaming, grilling and smoking. Eel is great simmered in stews, but try not to serve eel raw because it does not have good raw texture.

If you can purchase eel from a fish market, it's best bought alive, but if not, you can get it with skin or skinless, filleted or as steaks.

Freshwater mud mussel

Aboriginal name/s ngidjubany or gudjubay (Djabugay tribe, Kuranda, Far North Qld), kurruwul (Kija tribe, east Kimberley, WA)
Scientific name *Velesunio wilsonii*

Freshwater mud mussels can be found in the muddy banks of brackish and fresh waters, mainly billabongs, rivers, creeks and lakes. Freshwater mussels prefer warmer climates.

Like common green mussels, freshwater mud mussels grow in black, ear-shaped shells. An adult mussel can grow up to 8–12cm long. The shell features radial markings, similar to tree ring markings. It has a top and bottom that are joined by two very strong, white, sinew-like hinges. Inside, the shell is pearly white. It holds a soft, rubbery, muscular, compact mussel, which is said to be not as tasty as their saltwater relative. These mussels are also filter feeders and are very sensitive to pollution.

Traditional use Freshwater mussels were an important source of food for Aboriginal people. Middens containing large numbers of mussel shells are widespread alongside rivers and lakes. Women and young girls would search for freshwater mud mussels while the men watched for crocodiles. The women and girls would immerse themselves in the water of creeks or rivers and swim along the banks, using their hands to dig around the muddy banks until they found a hard sharp object, which they would then dig out. They would fill their dilly bags, coolamons or paperbark baskets with the mussels.

The flesh was eaten after roasting in hot coals or boiling in water. Freshwater mud mussels were one of the foods Aboriginal people ate when they were in mourning.

The shell of a freshwater mud mussel has a pretty, lustrous sheen and is sometimes called pearl-shell. The mussel shells were also used as tools for carving or cutting.

Other uses Freshwater mud mussels are not popular because they are not attractive to look at, do not have a palatable flavour and do not offer a marketable enticement to the commercial food industry. But to the Indigenous freshwater people, it will always be a valued food source, providing high levels of protein, zinc, iron and vitamin their bodies naturally need.

Freshwater mud mussels can be cooked to your liking and in the same way as green mussels: in a stir-fry or as part of a marinara using white wine, tomatoes, garlic and parsley. The best way to cook mussels is to put them directly on the hot coals until they open.

Freshwater prawn 🍴

Aboriginal name/s cherrabin (Bardi tribe, north of Broome, the
Kimberley, WA), jalijkel (Kija tribe, east Kimberley, WA)
Scientific name *Macrobrachium spp*

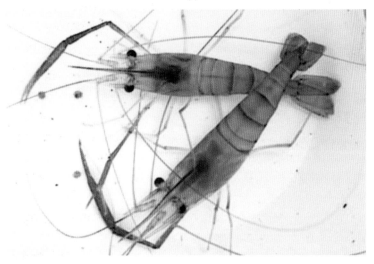

Freshwater prawns (also known as giant
freshwater prawns, freshwater shrimps and
inland crustaceans) are found in rivers, creeks
and billabongs, around rock ledges, under
leaves and in hollow logs. They live in the warm waters
throughout the northern regions of Australia, where they
are called cherrabins by the local Indigenous communities.
Cherrabins are related to prawns and crayfish. They look
very similar to prawns and crayfish, except that they have
long, slender nippers, which are bright blue. Cherrabins
can grow up to 15–30cm long and their body colour in the
water is green and blue, allowing them to be camouflaged
in freshwater environments. Their flesh is clear, almost

transparent, but when cooked it turns white and their shells turn bright orange. The texture of the meat is similar to crayfish, but freshwater prawns are not as tasty as saltwater shellfish.

Traditional use The people in the Kimberley regard cherrabin as a delicacy, and take pride in the hunting and gathering of it. Back in the days before cast nets, they would gather sticks and entwine them with a bit of string; they would tuck the bait tightly in the sticks so when the cherrabin swims in to get the bait, it is difficult for it to come back out because the sticks would trap it. The women and children would also sit in the water dangling red meat around their bodies and when the cherrabin would come to eat the bait, they would quickly grab them with their hands.

Cherrabin can be eaten by roasting them in hot ashes. They can also be used as bait when fishing, however most people think they are too tasty to be used as bait.

Other uses Nowadays cast nets, freshwater pots and dilly pots (netted traps) seem to be the easiest way to catch cherrabin. If using cast nets, spread or sprinkle chicken pellets in the water close to the bank and wait a few minutes before casting the nets. If using freshwater pots, people go crazy using all sorts of bait in the pots, from semi-boiled potatoes, tuna cans, soap bars, blocks of cheese and so on; when choosing your bait, please be

Freshwater prawn 🍴

mindful of what your bait is doing to the environment and how it would effect the other fish life in the water.

Cherrabin are best cooked whole (shell and all) on the hot coals, to maintain the flavours. Some people like to cook it in stir-fries with Asian flavours, or simply barbecue it or even boil it. Cherrabin are just starting to appear on restaurant menus, mainly advertised as a bush tukka cuisine.

Please be warned: The Northern Territory government has implemented a 'Great Territory lifestyle initiative' based on maintaining healthy and sustainable waterways, to ensure current and future generations can be enjoy the pleasures of fishing. This initiative is managed and monitored by the Fisheries Division and they have set limits on how many cherrabin you can have in your possession: the maximum is 30 per person, and female cherrabin carrying eggs must be returned to the water. There are also limits on how many freshwater pots can be used: a maximum of 5 freshwater pots or dilly pots per person.

Goanna 🍴➕

Aboriginal name/s karda (Noongar tribe, sout-west corner of WA), ganyal (Djabugay tribe, Kuranda, Far North Qld), kanyarrany (Kija tribe, east Kimberley, WA) **Scientific name** *Aranus varius*

There are 30 species of goannas in the world and 25 of them are found in Australia. Goannas (otherwise called Australian monitors) are giant, carnivorous lizards with sharp teeth and claws. They can grow as big as 2–3m long, and prey on birds, bird eggs and smaller mammals. Goannas are mostly dark in colouring with camouflage tones of cream, grey, black, brown and green.

Goannas are land animals and are found all over Australia, mostly in warmer climates. They reside underground, in ground burrows or hollow logs, but with their sharp claws goannas can also climb tall trees to get away from predators and to hunt for baby birds or eggs in nests.

Goanna 🍴 ➕

Traditional use Goannas are a delicacy amongst Aboriginal people. They feature strongly in dreamtime stories and as individual, family and clan spiritual totems. People who have an animal as a spiritual totem are responsible for the protection of that animal so it doesn't get over-hunted, and the spiritual stories attached to it. To dishonour a totemic animal can bring bad luck and bad energy to yourself, your family, your tribe or your land.

To hunt a goanna takes a lot of skill and energy; it involves tracking the goanna to find its burrow and then flushing it out to catch it. Goannas are extremely quick and if you miss it on the way out, you would have to be a very fast runner to chase it down. Most of the time, they run for the nearest tree, hollow log or burrow. If it climbs up a tree the only way to get it down is to stone it down, and if it runs into a hollow log the only way to get it out is to smoke it out by making a fire at one end to force the goanna out through the other end and have someone waiting to catch and kill it.

Aboriginal people cook goanna on hot coals: they make a fire and throw the goanna on the flames to burn off the tough layer of its skin; they let the fire burn down to coals then dig a hole in the middle of the hot coals, place the goanna inside and cover it with the hot coals for 30–40 minutes. The best parts of the goanna to eat are the legs and the tail. Goanna meat is white, and tastes like chicken breast, but a little drier. It is best eaten with the fat; this takes the experience to a whole other level, giving the meat the moisture and richness of the minerals in the fat. In western society eating fat is looked upon as unhealthy, but Aboriginal people eat everything, nothing goes to waste, and the fat is regarded as the prize of the animal because they believe it gives you energy and important natural minerals.

In the Wardandi Pibulmen of the Noongar nation, around the south-west coast of Western Australia, they call goanna 'karda' and they believe that when they hunt, catch and kill a goanna they must sing the *Janga* (spirit) from its body, then they break all its legs. If you do not sing the spirit from the body and break its legs it can bring *Mindich* (sickness) to your *Moort* (family), it also gets rigor mortis and comes to life in *Karla* (fire); essentially you are cooking it alive, which is *Warra* (bad).

Other uses Goanna oil was, and still is, an important bush medicine within Aboriginal communities. Its healing properties were used to rub on the skin as a natural moisturizer and to treat aching muscles and joints.

If you catch a goanna and want to cook it at home, it is best to cook it in the oven, or you can use the barbecue. Goanna is not available commercially.

Grasshopper 🍴

Aboriginal name/s muurruung (Wiradjuri tribe, central NSW), pirlpilji (east Kimberley, WA) **Scientific name** *Orthoptera, caelifera*

Grasshoppers can be found all over the world. They are interesting-looking insects with two big hind legs for jumping, and each leg has sharp defensive spikes on them. They have two pairs of narrow, transparent wings. They also have short antennae, prominent eyes, and two front and middle legs for balance.

Grasshoppers come out mainly in spring and summer, but they are most noticeable in autumn, when the large grasshoppers gather in groups, or swarms, causing plagues.

Traditional use Aboriginal people ate grasshoppers by placing them on hot coals to crisp up. Just after the wet season, grasshoppers are like a plague and when there are so many of them, it makes them easy to catch.

Women and children would have fun catching them. They would break off the legs so the grasshoppers could not hop away and then place them on the hot coals. Cooked this way, grasshoppers are crunchy, with a nutty flavour.

They also make great bait when fishing for barramundi.

Other uses A more contemporary way of cooking grasshopper is to collect 5–10 large grasshoppers, remove the legs and stir-fry them in hot peanut oil with garlic and light soy sauce. They are really very tasty!

Green ant 🍴 ➕

Aboriginal name/s djiliburay (Djabugay tribe, Kuranda, Far North Qld), wawalji (Kija tribe, east Kimberley, WA)
Scientific name *Oecophylla smaragdina*

Green ants (also known as weaver ants) are found throughout northern Australia and south-east Queensland, in the open woodland and rainforests. They are called green ants because they have green abdomens. Green ants crawl over everything, but can be seen in trees, building their nest by weaving and gluing leaves together.

These extremely aggressive ants pack a punch if you're bitten, but they will only bite if they feel threatened or scared. Their little bodies are yellow, and they have six thin legs and two antennae, which are as long as their middle and back legs.

Traditional use Aboriginal people swear by the medicinal properties of green ants. You can eat the ants individually by picking one up between your fingertips and biting off the green abdomen, then releasing the ant, giving you a tangy, mint flavour. The green abdomen acts as an antiviral agent for stomach aches and sore throats.

To get a more potent effect, find a nest and boil it in hot water. Once you have boiled it for 10 minutes, let the liquid cool down and then place a clean cloth over the bowl and pour the liquid into another bowl, catching the ants in the cloth. Then wrap the cloth up and squeeze the remaining juice out of the ants. Aboriginal people use the liquid to treat sore throats, aching bones and headaches by pouring it over their heads or drinking it like a tea, warm or cool. They also added honey to sweeten it as the mixture has a tangy, bitter flavour.

Other uses Green ants are the most valued insect eaten by humans because of its nutritional value. The ants are looked upon as a delicacy in countries like Thailand and Indonesia and are very expensive to buy.

Honey ant 🍴 ➕

Aboriginal name/s ngkwarle yerrampe (Arrernte tribe, central Australia, NT) **Scientific name** *Myrmecocystus*

Honey ants are predominantly found in the hot, dry, arid terrains of the western desert regions of Australia. They live deep underground. Trapped by their pea-sized abdomen, which is filled with honey, they are unable to reach the surface, but they serve as living larders for other ants. While honeybees collect and store their liquids in a nest or in a comb, honey ants are extremely unique as they store the liquid in their own bodies. They start off looking like normal ants. Worker ants feed them and they store the honeydew in their abdomens, which then grow into honeypots. A honey ant has a little red head, black ant-like body and six little legs; the honey pot is round and golden with two thick black bands on their backs.

Traditional use Aboriginal people from central Australia call honey ants *ngkwarle yerrampe*, which means 'honey ant dreaming'. Aboriginal women will look for a small hole on the ground, which indicates the entrance of the nest below. They then dig into the ant colony to find the nest. They have to be gentle and patient because sometimes the nests are buried deep in the ground. Once they find the nest, they carefully pluck the honey ants out to collect and distribute them among the other women and children. They only eat the back of the ant, the honeypot, and then they place the ant back in the nest to reproduce. It's hard work, but when you find the honey ants it makes it all the more rewarding.

Honey ants also play an important part in the dreaming stories of the Warlpiri people.

Other uses Mostly honey ants are used as a sweet little treat, but the honey is also good for sore throats and is used for medicinal purposes as the honey is nutritious and contains high levels of antiviral properties. It is also a good source of energy.

Kangaroo 🍴

Aboriginal name/s ganuurr (Wiradjuri tribe, central NSW), kere aherre (Arrernte tribe, central Australia, NT), malu (Anangu, Pitjantjatjara and Yankunytjatjara tribe, central Australia, NT), jarlangarnany (Kija tribe, east Kimberley, WA), gangurru (Guugu Yimithir tribe, Far North Qld)
Scientific name *Macropus rufus* (red kangaroo), *Macropus giganteus* (eastern grey kangaroo), *Macropus fuliginosus* (western grey kangaroo), *Macropus antilopinus* (antilopine kangaroo)

The kangaroo is a marsupial with large powerful hind legs, large feet for leaping and a long muscular tail for balance. Different types of kangaroo can be found all over Australia. Like most marsupials, female kangaroos have a pouch where joeys (baby kangaroos) complete their postnatal development; a joey can stay in its mother's pouch for up to 18 months. Kangaroo fur is well designed for the Australian climate, being water-, heat- and cold-proof. They have incredible long ears to be able to hear from great distances, as well as great smell sense to sniff out danger. They also have extremely long eyelashes and a very small mouth with perfect grass-eating teeth.

Kangaroos don't live in any particular habitat. They are comfortable hopping all over the countryside, looking for food and water. They can reach hopping speeds of up to 70km per hour for nearly 2kms. But kangaroos are nocturnal animals, so when they need to rest during the day, they will find a nice shady tree to sleep under with a landscape where they can graze on grass during the night.

There are four different species of kangaroo. The red kangaroo is the largest and is found mostly in the arid and semi-arid centre of Australia. A male can grow as tall as 2m, and weigh 90–100kg. The eastern grey kangaroo is mostly found on the east coast of Australia. The western grey kangaroo is found across the southern part of Australia. The male is small, weighing approximately 54kg as an adult. The last one is the antilopine kangaroo, which lives in the far northern parts of Australia, enjoying the grassy plains and woodlands.

Traditional use The word kangaroo originated from the Guugu Yimithir word *gangurru* and was recorded in a diary entry by Sir Joseph Banks as *kanguru*.

Kangaroos play an important part in the dreamtime stories of many Aboriginal language groups across Australia, and it has spiritual totemic significance for some tribes. The Arrernte people of central Australia call kangaroo *kere aherre* and the Anangu, Pitjantjatjara and Yankunytjatjara people also of the central Australia call kangaroo *malu*.

Kangaroo 🍴

Aboriginal men were the hunters of larger animals, especially kangaroo. They used weapons like the spear and woomera (which assisted the spear to be thrown faster, harder, more accurately and over longer distances). As with most bush tukka, every part of the kangaroo was used, nothing went to waste: from the meat, to the fur, and even the sinew, which was used to bind weapons and tools. Once killed and cooked, the kangaroo's warm blood would also be drained and shared amongst the men and boys of the tribe so that they could take on the strength, the speed and the wisdom of the animal.

Other uses Kangaroo meat is believed to be the leanest meat on the market. High in protein, low in fat and rich in iron, kangaroo meat is full of flavour. It should be cooked medium–rare, on a sizzling hotplate or barbecue, to retain its natural juices and flavour. Kangaroo meat works extremely well in all dishes and styles of cooking from stir-fries, slow-cooked stews, curries and casseroles, to kebabs, spaghetti sauce and roasts.

Kangaroo meat has become a commercial favourite; more and more restaurants are serving wonderful gourmet-style kangaroo dishes, but unfortunately people still have a reluctance to eat Skippy, from the well-loved Australian kids television series *Skippy, the Bush Kangaroo*.

Magpie goose

Aboriginal name/s djawadjawa dagi (Djabugay tribe, Kuranda, Far North Qld), gurrumattji (Raminging tribe, Arnhem Land, NT), ngarlakangarriny (Kija tribe, east Kimberley, WA) **Scientific name** *Anseranas semipalmata*

Magpie geese are large waterbirds that live around savannah and northern coastal parts of Australia, like the Kimberley regions in Western Australia, the Top End in the Northern Territory, and in Far North Queensland. A magpie goose is black from the top of its head to the base of its neck, and has black wings. Its body is covered in white feathers, with orange legs and beak. These classic birds can be found around wetlands, swamps, floodplains and cane paddocks, but they move around to different locations quite regularly during the dry season. They are also very noisy, quacking and communicating with each other all the time.

Traditional use The Ganalbingu, or Magpie Goose people, are the largest clan in central Arnhem Land. They have a respect for magpie geese and their spirit, as the magpie goose is part of the Ganalbingu dreaming. Magpie goose eggs and nests are sacred to the Ganalbingu people as they are seen as the resting place for the geese's souls. A ceremony called *Gurrbumgungu* is held when the first eggs are collected, to ensure that the geese will lay again.

The community also holds a welcome ceremony of the Gurrumba Mapu (goose eggs). New mothers in the tribe will paint themselves around their armpits with white ochre or clay to represent breast milk. Two men will dance the Goose dance with cooked eggs. They will break the shells and give them to the mothers and their babies, rubbing the eggs over the babies to ensure that they and their mothers will stay healthy during the infant years.

Aboriginal people of north central Arnhem Land cook magpie geese in a *Bundatharri* or *Yathalamara*: they make a fire on the hot coals, then they put paperbark leaves down and put the magpie geese on the leaves and then cover it with paperbark and sand until no steam is coming out, after 40 minutes they dust off the sand and remove the paperbark sheets to reveal steam-baked magpie geese.

Ngarlakangarriny is only found on Kija country (in the east Kimberley) during the wet season. The Kija name is based on the sound of the call of the magpie geese; they also make a honking noise.

Other uses People in Arnhem Land still hunt and eat magpie geese today and prefer to prepare and cook it in the traditional ways. Magpie geese have dark flesh, very similar to bush turkey meat but much more tender. Magpie geese have not reached the commercial food market, but the Aboriginal people of Arnhem Land treasure them.

Mangrove snail 🍴

Aboriginal name/s djidin or gudjubay (Djabugay tribe, Kuranda, Far North Qld) **Scientific name** *Nerita lineata*

Mangrove snails range in size from 1–2 cm at maturity. They can be found around rocky shores, reef rocks and mangrove vegetation, mostly in the northern regions of Australia. They are often found in large numbers, clustering together, near watermarks around mangrove roots.

The shell is rounded and durable, usually black or grey, with distinguished black stripes down the back; underneath it is smooth, with a tinge of yellow at the outer entrance of the shell. The snail is pale with thin black bands on its single foot, and long, thin, black tentacles which act as sensors to help them become aware of predators like birds, crabs or humans. When they sense danger, they retreat into their shells. Mangrove snails have a little door or lid that seals off the snail inside the shell to protect it against predators.

Mangrove snails are herbivores. They feed on algae growing on reef rocks and mangrove roots.

You can use mangrove snails for bait. They are particularly good bait for barramundi.

Traditional use Aboriginal people in the far north Northern Territory enjoy collecting mangrove snails (also known as periwinkles). They are best cooked on hot coals for 3–5 minutes, until you can see liquid bubbling from the entrance and when the lid begins to pop open. To access the snail, either crack the back of the shell or find a thin, sharp stick (like a toothpick) and peel the lid away, fishing out the snail at the same time. They can also be boiled in water for about 10 minutes.

Other uses Mangrove snails have not really hit the commercial food industry, but they offer the same delicacy as land snails, or escargot, that are served as cherished appetizers in France. Cooked in the same manner as escargot (fried or baked in garlic herb butter) gives these miniature morsels a delightful twist of decadence.

Mangrove worm 🍴

Aboriginal name/s latjin (Galiwin'ku tribe, Echo Island)
Scientific name *Teredo navalis*

Mangrove worms are found in rotted-out mangrove roots and logs, around the northern regions of Australia. These threadworm-looking molluscs are best found around low tide. Long, and grey and slimy in texture, mangrove worms delight in eating the centre of the rotten wood of mangrove trees and logs by using its sharp-beaked head to chew through the cork fibres. They like the coastal saltwater environments in warmer weather, and can grow as long as 40cm.

Traditional use Mangrove worms are highly regarded by the coastal Yolngu people in far north Arnhem Land in the Northern Territory. The Yolngu enjoy, and are very good at, tracking through the mangroves and finding dead broken logs or dead roots where they can harvest mangrove worms nesting inside. Mangrove worms are mostly eaten raw.

Other uses Mangrove worms are not the type of bush tukka you will find on the menu in a restaurant. They should be kept and eaten in their natural habitat, but in saying that, these slimy little morsels are a delicacy to Aboriginal people, and taste very similar to oysters. Mangrove worms are also a rich source of protein and iron.

Mud crab 🍴

Aboriginal name/s djindjalma (Yithuwa Madarrpa tribe, north-east Arnhem Land, NT) **Scientific name** *Scylla serrata* (green mud crab), *Scylla olivaea* (brown mud crab)

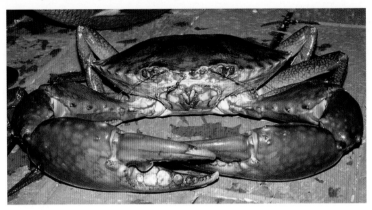

 Mud crabs are abundant in estuaries, mangrove swamps, creeks and rivers, and in more protected environments like under mangroves roots, in mud and water pools, and in burrows. Two species of mud crabs are found in Australia: green mud crabs and brown mud crabs. Throughout north-west Western Australia, the top of the Northern Territory, Queensland and New South Wales, recreational fishers can harvest mud crabs by hand (depending on locations within each state or territory), using traps, traditional spears, crab hooks, dilly pots and lift nets.

A mature green mud crab can grow up to 30cm wide, and weigh 2.5kg. The brown mud crab grows to half the size of a green mud crab: 15cm wide, and weighs 1.5kg.

Female crabs are protected; if you catch a Jenny crab (as a female crab is called) you must release it back into the mud or water. You can easily tell a Jenny crab by its abdominal flaps, which are much broader than the male or 'buck' abdominal flaps. Also, when Jenny crabs reach their mature cycle, their claws are a lot smaller than a male crab. Do your research before you go mud crabbing to avoid heavy fines if you're caught with Jenny crabs.

When catching mud crab by hand, be very careful as their nippers can cut through almost anything and can certainly take off your fingers. It is best to approach a mud crab from behind and hold its body down using a stick and then grab the back swimmer-legs in a firm lock. The nippers will rise to try and attack you, but they don't go backwards so you can catch it this way without getting hurt.

Traditional use Aboriginal people have enjoyed mud crab hunting for thousands of years. The first sign of when mud crabs are ready to be hunted is when the bark on the eucalypts starts to peel away from the tree. Although the method of hunting for mud crabs has advanced somewhat, it is still a lot of fun for the whole family!

Aboriginal people used to catch mud crabs by hand or using a stick or spears to force them from their burrows. Hunting this way takes a lot of energy: walking through the thick, wet mud of sandfly- and mosquito-infested mangroves, and climbing over the entwined mangrove

Mud crab 🍴

roots. It was and is hard work, so they only took the respectful amount needed to feed their families as they were aware they still had to carry the heavy mud crabs back the way they had come.

The traditional way to cook mud crabs is on hot coals. Some people may think this is cruel, but this has been a cooking method for thousands of years. Cooking foods directly on the coals is a much healthier way to cook because it maintains the nutrients of the food which can be lost through other cooking methods.

Every part of the mud crab is eaten. The best part is what Indigenous people call 'the soup'. This is the guts of the crab: the yellow and white creamy substance you find under the main shell when you peel it open. This creamy substance is rich in protein, vitamins and minerals including zinc and iron. The claws are also very yummy to eat because they have a different texture to the rest of the body, and nothing is wasted except the gills in the body, which are grey in colour and look like sharp fingers.

Other uses Mud crabs are highly sought after. They are sold live in markets, fishmongers and supermarkets. Of all the bush foods, besides oysters and mussels, mud crabs have become a fashionable dinner experience in many commercial restaurants around the world. Mud crabs have hit the commercial food industry in a big way and there are concerns that mud crabs are being over-fished in Australian waters. In the Northern Territory and Queensland mud-crab farms are a promising opportunity of selling both to the domestic and overseas markets.

Mud crabs can be cooked in so many ways. The most popular dish is chilli mud crabs. You can experiment using mud crabs in curries, stir-fries and even making crab cakes.

Mud whelk 🍴➕

Aboriginal name/s marrkika (Iwaidja tribe, Cobourg Peninsula, NT)
Scientific name *Telescopium telescopium*

Mud whelks (also known as long bums) prefer the warm climates of Northern Australia, and can be found at low tide, living in muddy banks around mangrove vegetation and roots, and near watermarks. They are often found clustering together in large numbers. They have long, cone-shaped shells, which are brown with a creamy spiral pattern. The shells have a large opening at the wide end of the cone and can grow up to 11cm long.

Mud whelks belong to the same family as the mangrove snail but mud whelks have a more conical shell. These shells however, sometimes house hermit crabs, so you must be careful when gathering and cooking them. You can tell that a mud whelk lives inside the shell by the colour of the inside shell which should be light blue.

The mud whelk itself is the most amazing bright blue colour that you will ever see in a snail.

When collecting mud whelks, you're best to take a bucket, as they are quite large in size. When you cook mud whelks on the hot coals, it's best to place them sharp end down with the open end sticking out of the coals; this way the whole snail will cook thoroughly.

To get the snail out of the shell you need to poke it with a sharp metal object. But there is a trick to it, as the snail will break if you're not careful and gentle in pulling it out. Another way is to get a hard object and break the side of the shell after it has been cooked (when it is easier to break open), then you can fish out the snail, splitting the body in half.

Traditional use Mud whelks are a delicacy among Aboriginal people. Most Aboriginal people cook mud whelk shells on hot coals or boil them in hot water.

Aboriginal people eat mud whelks to fight viral and chest infections because of its rich mineral content.

Other uses Mud whelks have not reached the commercial market as they are not seen as an attractive bush tukka, and are very hard to harvest. The colour of the snail would also turn a lot of people off, as they are not used to eating anything that is curly and bright blue; it does take time to get used to.

Mud whelk 🍴 ➕

The taste of mud whelks is quite salty. They are a rich source of sodium, iron and protein. You should not eat too much however, because these snails can give you diarrhoea if you eat too many.

Native milky oyster 🍴

Aboriginal name/s bandin (Djabugay tribe, Kuranda, Far North Qld),
Scientific name *Saccostrea cucullata*

There are many species of oysters, but native milky oysters should not be confused with pearl oysters which are not edible. Native milky oysters can be found growing in huddles or clusters on anything solid from mangrove roots to reef shelves to rocky walls. They prefer to live in sheltered surroundings where the surface water is warm enough for spawning in summer. They can also be found growing in most estuaries and bays along the northern, eastern and southern coasts of Australia. Some oysters grow up to 8–12cm in size and, if you're lucky, you can find oysters the size of a dinner plate!

Native milky oysters grow in an ear-shaped little cup or shell, with a lid, but they vary in size depending on the surface on which they grow, such as rocks, mangroves,

Native milky oyster

wooden or concrete pilons, or around boat ramps and jetties. The shells are generally grey with jagged, waved edges around the lip of the lid, which is generally shut tight. Inside the shell, the oyster body is cream but the gills are black and grey, and the shell on the inside is white with a smooth, porcelain surface.

Native milky oysters are easy to harvest or collect off the rocks, but they are hard to collect without entirely destroying them. You can neatly scrape the oysters off the rocks with a screwdriver and a hammer. If you don't have these tools, then find a hard, longish rock with a pointy end to use as a hammer to crack the oysters open. Be careful not to crack the oysters directly on top and squash the lid onto it, but to tap them from the side; you will see how the lids start to open. Once you have loosened the lid, remove the oyster from its shell. This can be tricky because the oyster muscles are very strong. You can eat the oyster raw, straight from the shell, or try and crack the whole shell off the rocks and then cook it on hot coals.

Traditional use Native milky oysters are abundant bush tukka. With easy harvesting at low tide, collecting oysters is fun for Aboriginal women and children, and it does not take up a lot of energy. Oysters have been a staple food for coastal saltwater Aboriginal people for thousands of years.

Other uses Native milky oysters are a huge commercial bush tukka and restaurants have many ways of serving them. Oysters in the western world are very expensive and highly prized. Restaurants buy their oysters directly from oyster farms – that way they know they are getting healthy, good-quality oysters. Restaurants seek closed oysters. They shuck or open them freshly in their kitchens using special oyster knives and heavy-duty gloves to prevent any oyster cuts, that way the oysters are fresh.

The wonderful thing about oysters is that they can be eaten raw or cooked. There are many creative ways to cook oysters, but the most common ways are oysters Kilpatrick or served with a cheesy Mornay sauce.

Oysters have been proven to have high levels of zinc, calcium and iron, as well as vitamins A and B12, and studies have found them to be most nutritious when eaten raw.

Saltwater mud mussel 🍴 ➕

Aboriginal name/s djulwa (Djabugay tribe, Kuranda, Far North Qld)
Scientific name *Polymesoda coaxans*

Saltwater mud mussels prefer saltwater mud flats and mangrove environments; they like warm, dry climates and can be found at low tide, predominantly around the north-western and north-eastern parts of Australia. The length of a mature mud mussel is 8–12cm. The shell features radial markings, similar to tree ring markings. Mud mussels range in colour from black at the tip of the shell, to brown and white around the base of the shell. Inside, the mussel is quite fleshy, but this decreases to the size of a 20-cent piece when cooked.

To find saltwater mud mussels, look for evidence of large, black shells in the mud, or small holes on the surface of the mud through which the mussels breathe. The mussels are usually imbedded deep in mangrove mud flats, so you have to dig in the mud with your hands to find them, but if you're lucky, you will find them on the surface of the mud as they make their way across the mud to find another home. You can also find mussels in dry, cracked mud: look out for a small straight opening, about 25mm long, slightly covered in the mud. They're not easy to find, but once you know what you're looking for, you will start to see the landscape differently.

Traditional use Saltwater mud mussels are a delicacy for the northern Arnhem Land Yolngu people. Although different tribes call them different names, the hunting and cooking techniques are pretty much the same. After a day of gathering the mussels in the mangroves, they find a nice shady tree, light a fire, and place the mussels on the hot coals. After about 5 minutes the shells start to open, indicating that the mussels are ready to eat.

Another way the Yolngu people like to cook mud mussels is to boil them in hot water. This gives the mussels a rubbery texture, but a more creamy taste. The Yolngu people also drink the warm, salty water the mussels were cooked in to get the rich minerals from the mussels which helps the body fight colds and other viruses.

Other uses Mud mussels are very different to commercial green mussels: mud mussels are not as attractive to look at and do not offer a marketable enticement to the commercial food industry. But to the Indigenous saltwater people, they always be a valued food source, providing high levels of protein, zinc, iron and vitamins that their bodies need.

Witchetty grub 🍴

Aboriginal name/s maku lunki (Pitjantjatjara tribe, central NT), ilykuwara (Yankunytjatjara tribe, central NT) **Scientific name** *Endoxyla leucomochla*

It takes a brave soul to try eating witchetty grubs without gagging. People think all Aboriginal people eat the grub and that it can be found everywhere. But the truth is, bush tukka is specific to the types of country you have been brought up in, so if you were born in the desert, then you would most likely have been raised and taught to eat witchetty grubs.

Witchetty grubs are an all-time favourite bush tukka. They are the wood-eating larvae of a moth. They are found eating through the roots of river red gum and blood wood trees in the central deserts of Australia.

Witchetty grubs are white with a yellow head and soft skin. They grow as fat as 1.5cm thick, and as long as 12cm.

Traditional use These grubs are a staple of the diets of Aboriginal people in the desert. Although it's hard work digging for the grubs, only the women dig for them. When they have collected enough, they light a small fire and throw the grubs onto the hot coals and cover them with hot ash to cook for about 5 minutes. The grubs have a nutty flavour, and a texture very similar to warm scrambled eggs, but if eaten raw the grubs are soft and slimy with a sweet flavour. It's best to eat the grubs whole, in one go.

Other uses Witchetty grubs are a famous bush tukka that everyone refers to when bush tukka is mentioned. Commercial chefs use witchetty grubs to promote bush tukka in their restaurants. Everyone should try them at least once in their life. For the more squeamish stomachs witchetty grubs are best eaten cooked, which is a simple process of lightly frying them in a frying pan, with or without oil, for approximately 5–10 minutes, turning continuously to allow it to cook evenly.

Recipes

Lemon myrtle rustic damper

Ingredients

3 cups self-raising flour

pinch of salt

80g butter, melted

30g bush tomatoes

30g dried lemon myrtle leaves, crushed

¾ cup warm water

Method

1. Preheat the oven to 200°C, and grease a large baking tray well with oil or butter.

2. Combine the flour, salt, butter, bush tomatoes and lemon myrtle leaves in a large mixing bowl and, using your fingers, rub all the ingredients together until it resembles a crumbly mixture.

3. Slowly add the water to the mixture and stir well with a large mixing spoon, until the mixture starts to blend together, adding small amounts of water if the mixture gets too dry.

4. Once the mixture becomes like dough, use your hands to knead it into a firm dough. The dough should be smooth, not sticky. Place the dough onto a dry, well-floured surface and knead gently for 2–3 minutes, folding the dough until smooth and firm.

5. Shape the dough into a disc and place it onto your baking tray. Take a sharp knife and make shallow cuts into the dough, like cutting a pizza, and sprinkle with flour.

6. Bake for 30–40 minutes, until golden brown and cooked through in the middle. You can test this by piercing a skewer through the middle; if the skewer comes out clean, it is ready. Transfer to a wire rack and let cool for 5 minutes. Slice and spread with butter, jam or honey.

Makes 1 large damper, serves 10–12 people

Traditionally this damper was cooked in a hot cast-iron pot called a camp oven, which had a lid to contain the heat. The camp oven was put on a fire with hot coals underneath, around and on top of it to create even heat. It was also cooked in a ground oven where a hole was dug and hot coals placed in the hole, and then the camp oven was placed in the hole, with hot coals placed all around it to create an even-heated oven. Dampers were traditionally made out bush and are best enjoyed with tea or stews. The original dampers were just flour, salt and water. The other ingredients came later to add flavour.

Native bush dukkah

Ingredients

25g dried bush tomatoes, whole or crushed

25g dried lemon myrtle leaves, whole leaves or crushed

10g wattleseeds, whole or crushed

10g bush mountain pepper, whole or crushed

10g sea salt, whole or crushed

100g roasted almonds, whole or crushed

Native bush dukkah

. . . .

Method

1. If you are using whole ingredients, put the bush tomatoes, lemon myrtle leaves, wattle seeds, bush mountain pepper and sea salt into a food processor or blender, and grind coarsely. Add the roasted almonds, and grind a little more, until powdered to your liking.

2. If you are using crushed ingredients, put all the ingredients into a sealable sandwich bag and shake well. Crush the roasted almonds and add to the mixture, combining all ingredients well.

Best served with Australian olive oil and fresh rustic bread.

Makes 200g

Bunya nut pesto

Ingredients

1 cup bunya nuts, cooked, peeled and shucked

½ bunch basil leaves

½ bunch rocket

4 garlic cloves

1 chilli

2 tablespoons lemon juice

¼ cup oil

Bunya nut pesto

Bunya nut preparation

1. Place bunya nuts in a pot of boiling water with a pinch of salt. Boil for half an hour, or until the water turns brown and you see the tip of the nuts open slightly.

2. To open or shuck a bunya nut, place a small knife at the tip, where it is slightly open, and cut ¾ into the shell. Once you have made a cut, you can then peel the shell off to reveal the nut inside.

Method

1. Shuck all bunya nuts and place in a food processor and process until slightly crushed. Add basil, rocket, garlic and chilli, and process until all ingredients are combined.

2. Add lemon juice and oil, and process a little more to mix through.

Serve with crusty bread or crackers. Or you can use the pesto in pasta, fish, chicken or pork dishes; this pesto is especially great for marinating chicken and seafood. You can also pour the pesto into a jar and use at your own leisure. It will keep up to 2–3 weeks.

Makes 250g

Stir-fried grasshoppers

Ingredients

4 tablespoons peanut oil

1 teaspoon sesame oil

2 tablespoons light soy sauce

1 large brown onion, diced

4 garlic cloves, crushed

1 large red chilli, deseeded (optional)

2 shallots, sliced

10–15 large brown grasshoppers, legs removed

Method

1. Heat peanut oil, sesame oil and soya sauce in a wok.

2. Add the onion, garlic, chilli and shallots, and fry until the onion is slightly transparent.

3. Add the grasshoppers and cook until they turn slightly brown.

Serve immediately.

Serves 4

Chilli and bush tomato mud crabs

Ingredients

Mud crabs

2 tablespoons peanut oil

1 large onion, finely diced

4 garlic cloves, finely crushed

2 teaspoons ginger, finely crushed

2 mud crabs

Chilli sauce

400g tin crushed tomatoes

½ cup sweet chilli sauce

½ cup tomato paste

2 tablespoons fish sauce

1 tablespoon palm sugar

2 lemon myrtle leaves (fresh or dried)

2 tablespoons crushed bush tomatoes

1 tablespoon white vinegar

5 fresh basil leaves, finely sliced

Method

Mud crabs

1. To prepare the mud crabs, lift the top of the crab shell from the rest of the body, then remove and discard the long, grey lungs. Rinse the crab well and cut it in half down the middle, and then in half again, separating the legs.

2. In a large wok, heat the peanut oil. Add the onions, garlic and ginger. Toss until onion starts to brown.

3. Add crab quarters and toss until the crab turns a slight orange colour, remove from the wok.

. . . .

Chilli Sauce

1. Add the tin of tomatoes, chilli sauce, tomato paste, fish sauce, palm sugar, lemon myrtle leaves, bush tomatoes and white vinegar to the wok and stir well. Leave until sauce starts to bubble, then return the mud crabs to the wok. Stir well and bring to the boil.

2. Cover and let simmer for 10 minutes, until all crab pieces turn bright orange.

3. Sprinkle with finely chopped basil for presentation.

Serve with rice or crusty bread.

Serves 4

Creamy garlic cherrabin

Ingredients

500g fresh cherrabin (freshwater prawns)

2 tablespoons oil

50g butter

1 large brown onion, diced

4 garlic cloves, crushed

1 large red chilli, deseeded (optional)

2 shallots, diced

500g cooking cream

2 tablespoons chicken stock

Creamy garlic cherrabin

Method

1. Peel shells off cherrabins, including the heads.

2. Add oil and butter to a frying pan on high heat. Once hot, add the onion, garlic, chilli and shallots, and fry until the onion is slightly transparent.

3. Add the cherrabin and cook until they turn slightly orange in colour.

4. Add cream and chicken stock, and bring to the boil. Once boiling, reduce the flame and cook for another 5 minutes, until cherrabin are cooked well (they will turn white in colour and firm in texture), but not overcooked.

Serve on a bed of jasmine rice.

(Note: this dish is best eaten fresh.)

Serves 6

Mangrove snails with garlic butter

Ingredients

125g butter

1 onion, finely chopped

4 garlic cloves, finely chopped

2 lemon myrtle leaves (fresh or dried)

½ cup white wine

1 tablespoon brown sugar

1kg mangrove snails or periwinkles

½ cup fresh parsley, finely chopped

Mangrove snails with garlic butter

Method

1. Melt butter in a large pot. Add onion, garlic and lemon myrtle leaves to the melted butter, and cook until the onion becomes transparent.

2. Add the wine and sugar, and bring to the boil. Then add the mangrove snails or periwinkles and parsley. Stir well. Cover and simmer for 10 minutes.

Serve on a bed of rice or spaghetti with crusty bread.

Serves 6

Mountain bush pepper and desert lime whole baked barramundi

Ingredients

1 whole barramundi, scaled and gutted

½ teaspoon mountain bush pepper, crushed

4 tablespoons of light soya sauce

6 desert limes, sliced

Large knob of ginger, julienned

3 garlic cloves, crushed

1 red chilli, deseeded and thinly sliced

3 spring onions, thinly sliced

Mountain bush pepper and desert lime whole baked barramundi

. . . .

Method

1. Preheat oven at 250°C for 20 minutes, then turn down to 180°C.

2. Rinse your barramundi and dry well. Make 3 even slashes on both sides and sprinkle with mountain bush pepper.

3. Lay a sheet of baking paper on a tray and place the barramundi in the center. Pour soya sauce over the fish and place the thin slices of desert lime, ginger, garlic, red chilli and spring onions over the flesh.

4. Once the barramundi is dressed up, grab the corners of the baking paper and bring to the center. Fold over to create a parcel, ensuring you leave a little hole to allow for the steaming process.

5. Cook for 25–35 minutes. If your fish is larger, cook for 35–45 minutes or until the fish flesh turns white.

Serve on a bed of rice or with a salad of your choice.

Serves 2

Camp-oven roasted bush turkey and vegetables

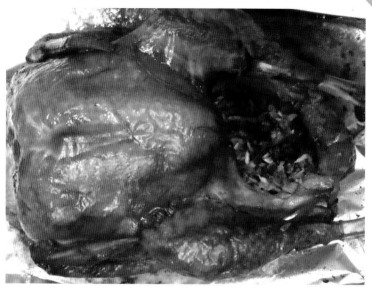

Ingredients

1 bustard bird or bush turkey

oil

salt and pepper

6–10 lemon myrtle leaves (fresh or dried)

4 potatoes, peeled and cut into quarters

4 garlic cloves, whole

3 onions, cut into quarters

2 large tomatoes, cut into quarters

Camp-oven roasted bush turkey and vegetables

Method

1. Pluck the turkey and remove the guts.

2. Smear oil all over the turkey and season well with salt, pepper and lemon myrtle leaves.

3. Grease a large camp oven well with oil. Wrap the turkey in foil to keep it moist, and then place it into the camp oven.

4. If the turkey is small enough, you can place the potatoes, garlic, onions and tomatoes around it in the camp oven. Otherwise, you will need to bake the vegetables in a separate camp oven.

5. Place the camp oven on the coals and shovel more hot coals on top and around the camp oven.

6. Cook for approximately 35–45 minutes (for a small turkey, or 40–50 minutes if a large turkey), or until the turkey is cooked through and the skin is a lovely golden brown.

Serves 8–10

Lemon myrtle slow-cooked kangaroo

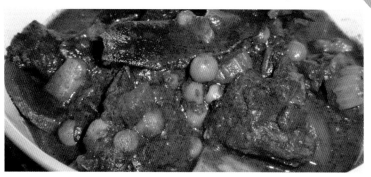

Ingredients

1kg kangaroo fillet, diced

½ cup flour

2 tablespoons olive oil

1 onion, chopped

1 garlic clove, crushed

2 carrots, chopped

2 potatoes, cut into large cubes

3 stalks celery (including leaves), chopped

400g tin crushed tomatoes

2 teaspoons lemon myrtle leaves (fresh or dried)

½ teaspoon bush mountain pepper

¼ cup red wine

2 tablespoons beef stock

1 cup peas

Method

1. Lightly cover the kangaroo chunks in flour.

2. Heat oil in a large pot. Fry onion and garlic until soft, then add flour-covered kangaroo and fry until browned.

3. Add carrots, potatoes and celery and stir until the vegetables soften. If the ingredients stick to the pot, use a bit of water to stop them from burning.

4. Add tomatoes, lemon myrtle, mountain pepper, red wine and beef stock to the pot. Add enough water to cover ingredients and stir well. Bring to the boil.

5. Turn heat to low and simmer for 2–3 hours until the meat is tender. Add the peas and cook for a few more minutes.

6. Thicken if necessary with a little cornflour mixed with water. Adjust seasoning to taste.

Serve with mashed potato or steamed rice.

Serves 6

Curried crocodile and potato mash

Ingredients

Curried crocodile

2 tablespoons oil

1 large onion, diced

2 garlic cloves, crushed

500g crocodile sausages

2 carrots, thinly sliced

2 sticks celery, thinly sliced

6 lemon myrtle leaves (fresh or dried)

2 tablespoons dry curry powder

Curried crocodile and potato mash

400g tin diced tomatoes

1 teaspoon brown sugar

1 tablespoon chicken stock

½ cup water

Potato mash

4 large potatoes, peeled and diced

1 tablespoon butter

dash of milk

pinch of salt

Method

Curried crocodile

1. Heat the oil in a pot. Once the oil is hot, fry the onion, garlic, sausages, carrots, celery and lemon myrtle leaves until the onion softens and sausages brown.

2. Add curry powder, tinned tomatoes, brown sugar and chicken stock, and stir well, until ingredients are mixed together. Add water if the mixture is dry.

3. Cook for 5–6 minutes, then take the crocodile sausages out and dice evenly. Return them to the frying pan.

4. When sausages are fully cooked through (they will be white in colour and firm to the touch), remove from the heat.

Potato mash

1. Boil diced potatoes until soft. Drain water, then add butter, milk and salt to potatoes and mash to your liking.

Serves 4

Traditional baked cheesecake with conkerberry and blueberry syrup

Ingredients

Cheesecake

275g Anzac biscuits

70g butter, melted

250g cream cheese

150g sour cream

75g caster sugar

2 eggs

seeds from 1 vanilla bean, or 1½ teaspoons
vanilla essence

Syrup

1 cup fresh conkerberries (for a sweet flavour, remove grape-size seeds from berries)

1 cup fresh or frozen blueberries

¾ cup caster sugar

¼ cup water

pinch of cinnamon

½ teaspoon vanilla essence

Method

Cheesecake

1. Preheat the oven to 190°C, and grease a 25cm springform cake tin well.

2. Add Anzac biscuits and melted butter to a food processor, and process until a smooth mixture forms. Spread the biscuit mixture evenly around the base of the cake tin, and press down on the mixture to ensure there are not gaps in the base. Cover the tin with cling wrap and place in the fridge.

3. In a mixing bowl, place the cream cheese, sour cream, caster sugar, eggs and vanilla essence and mix well, until all ingredients are combined – for the best results place the mixture into a food processor and process until it is smooth and creamy.

4. Pour the cheese mixture on top of the biscuit base and spread evenly. Place the cheesecake into the oven and bake for 1 hour. When cooked, turn the oven off but leave the cheesecake in the oven with the door slightly ajar until it cools down, this will help prevent it from cracking.

5. Once cooled, remove the cheesecake from the oven and place in the fridge for 4 hours, until chilled. Then remove the cheesecake from the cake tin and gently drizzle the berry syrup over the cheesecake.

Syrup

1. Put conkerberries, blueberries, caster sugar and water in a small saucepan over medium heat and bring to the boil, stirring gently at all times. Once boiling slightly, reduce heat.

2. Add cinnamon and vanilla essence to the syrup and stir gently until the syrup thickens. If the sauce is too thick, add water to thin it to your liking.

3. Once it reaches a syrup-like consistency, remove from heat. Allow syrup to cool to room temperature. Drizzle over cheesecake when ready to serve.

Serves 6

Bush passionfruit and gooseberry fruit salad

Ingredients

2 bananas

1 orange

1 red apple

1 pear

2 kiwifruit

10–15 native gooseberries

10–20 bush passionfruits (careful not to squash them)

Method

1. Peel bananas and orange and cut into whatever size you prefer.

2. Cut the apple, pear and kiwifruit into whatever size you prefer.

3. Place all the cut fruit and the gooseberries in a large bowl and toss gently.

4. Add the passionfruit, whole or squeeze the seeds over your salad and toss before serving.

You don't have to limit yourself to these ingredients. You can use whatever fruits are in season.

Serves 6

Caramelised cluster figs and ice-cream

Ingredients

5–10 cluster figs

2 tablespoons salted butter

2 tablespoons brown sugar

1 lemon peel

pinch of cinnamon powder

Method

1. Wash the figs and remove the stems. Cut in half.

2. Melt butter and brown sugar in a fry pan. Add lemon peel and cinnamon to create a sugar sauce.

3. Add the figs and cook for approximately 1–2 minutes or until figs turn a soft brown colour.

Serve with ice-cream flavour of your choice.

Serves 4–6

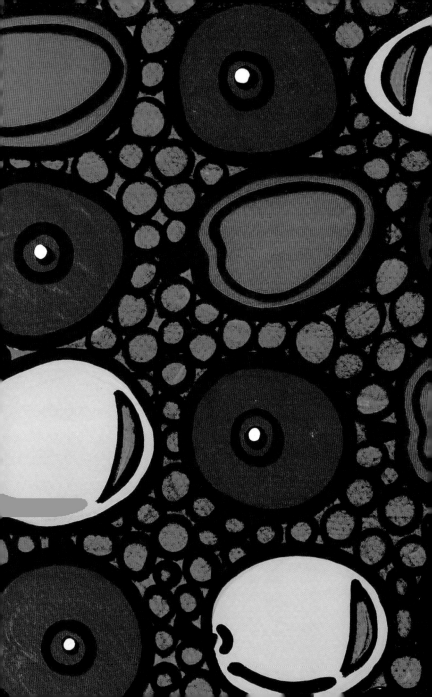

Where to buy bush tukka

You can purchase bush tukka from the following websites:

Australian BushFoods
www.ausbushfoods.com/oldmag/Products/bushfood_baskets.htm

Bush Tucker Recipes
http://bushtuckerrecipes.com

Bush Tucker Shop
www.bushtuckershop.com

Bushfood Sensations
http://bushfoodsensations.net

Chillingham Bush Tucker
www.chillinghambushtucker.com.au

Dreamtime Kullilla Art
www.kullillaart.com.au

Native Tastes of Australia
http://tasteaustralia.biz

Oz Tukka
www.oztukka.com.au

Taste Australia
www.bushfoodshop.com.au

Witjuti Grub Bushfood Nursery
www.witjutigrub.com.au

Index

Note: Types of bush tukka are shown in **bold**; *italic* entries refer to recipes; **bold** page numbers refer to recipe ingredients.

Acknowledgements

The publisher would like to acknowledge the following individuals and organisations:

Editorial manager
Melissa Krafchek

Project manager and editor
Alison Proietto

Cartography
Bruce McGurty, Claire Johnston

Design
Penny Black Design

Layout
Megan Ellis

Index
Mac McMaster

Illustrations
Bronwyn Bancroft

Pre-press
Splitting Image

Photography credits
Page xxii and xxiv Paul Thomsen; 106 Broken Hill City Council/Destination New South Wales; 128 Suzy Bennett/Alamy

Explore Australia Publishing Pty Ltd
Ground Floor, Building 1,
658 Church Street, Richmond, VIC 3121

Explore Australia Publishing Pty Ltd is a division of Hardie Grant Publishing Pty Ltd

hardie grant publishing

Published by Explore Australia Publishing Pty Ltd, 2014

Concept, maps, form and design © Explore Australia Publishing Pty Ltd, 2014

Text © Samantha Martin, 2014
Illustrations © Bronwyn Bancroft, 2014

A Cataloguing-in-Publication entry is available from the catalogue of the National Library of Australia at www.nla.gov.au

The maps in this publication incorporate data © Commonwealth of Australia (Geoscience Australia), 2006. Geoscience Australia has not evaluated the data as altered and incorporated within this publication, and therefore gives no warranty regarding accuracy, completeness, currency or suitability for any particular purpose.

Disclaimer
While every care is taken to ensure the accuracy of the data within this product, the owners of the data (including the state, territory and Commonwealth governments of Australia) do not make any representations or warranties about its accuracy, reliability, completeness or suitability for any particular purpose and, to the extent permitted by law, the owners of the data disclaim all responsibility and all liability (including without limitation, liability in negligence) for all expenses, losses, damages, (including indirect or consequential damages) and costs which might be incurred as a result of the data being inaccurate or incomplete in any way and for any reason.

ISBN-13 9781741174038

10 9 8 7 6 5 4 3 2 1

Printed and bound in China by 1010 Printing International Ltd

Publisher's note: Every effort has been made to ensure that the information in this book is accurate at the time of going to press. The publisher welcomes information and suggestions for correction or improvement. Email: info@exploreaustralia.net.au

Publisher's disclaimer: The publisher cannot accept responsibility for any errors or omissions. The representation on the maps of any road or track is not necessarily evidence of public right of way. The publisher cannot be held responsible for any injury, loss or damage incurred during travel. It is vital to research any proposed trip thoroughly and seek the advice of relevant state and travel organisations before you leave.

www.exploreaustralia.net.au
Follow us on Twitter: @ExploreAus
Find us on Facebook: www.facebook.com/exploreaustralia